Senior Academy

Computer Skills for Seniors

Word 2007 Basics

AN INTRODUCTION
TO MICROSOFT OFFICE WORD 2007

Word 2007 Basics

V808

Prepared by Ludwig Keck

Website: www.SeniorAcademy.org

Microsoft, Windows, Windows XP, Windows Vista, as well as other Microsoft products referenced in this book are either registered trademarks or trademarks of Microsoft Corporation in the United States and/or other countries.

Microsoft product screen shots reprinted with permission from Microsoft Corporation.

Other product and company names mentioned herein may be trademarks of their respective owners.

Materials, shown for illustrative purposes, contain attribution and source information.

Table of Contents

Introduction vi

1. WORD 2007 OVERVIEW 1.1
Getting Started.. 1.3
The Ribbon 1.5
The Office Button 1.7
Opening a Document 1.9
Viewing a Document 1.11
Moving Around in a Document... 1.13
Help 1.15
Lesson One Review Questions 1.17

2. ENTERING TEXT 2.1
Entering Text.. 2.3
Typing Text 2.5
Formatting Text.. 2.7
Correcting Text... 2.9
AutoCorrect – The Automatic Helper 2.11
More AutoCorrect Features 2.13
Automatic Bullets and Numbered Lists 2.15
Lesson Two Review Questions.. 2.17

3. CREATING, SAVING AND MANAGING FILES 3.1
Creating a Document 3.3
Finding a Saved Document 3.5
Saving as a New Document... 3.7
The Save Command 3.9
Moving Files 3.11
Organizing Files and Folders 3.13
Deleting a File or Folder 3.13

Creating a New Folder..3.15

Moving Files 3.17

Lesson Three Review Questions 3.19

4. MODIFYING TEXT 4.1

Cursor and Pointer 4.3

Selecting Text 4.5

Cut, Copy and Paste 4.9

Cut, Copy, Paste – Right-Click Method 4.9

Show/Hide Formatting Symbols 4.11

Cut, Copy and Paste – Using Icons 4.13

Cut, Copy Past – Using Shortcut Keys 4.15

Dragging Text 4.17

Text Alignment 4.19

Lesson Four Review Questions 4.21

5. MORE ON THE HOME TAB...5.1

Open Document – from Recent Lists 5.3

More Paragraph Formatting 5.5

Create a List as You Type 5.7

Styles 5.9

Find and Replace 5.11

Lesson Five Review Questions 5.15

6. THE INSERT AND REVIEW TABS...6.1

The Insert Tab 6.3

Inserting Pictures 6.5

Inserting Drawings and Shapes 6.7

WordArt 6.9

Text Box...6.11

Tables 6.11

The Review Tab 6.13

Spelling and Grammar Checking 6.15

Style Checking 6.17

Odds and Ends 6.18

Lesson Six Review Questions 6.21

7. THREE TABS: PAGE LAYOUT, VIEW AND REFERENCES 7.1

Page Layout 7.3

Viewing Your Document 7.7

The Reference Tab 7.9

Lesson Seven Review Questions 7.17

8. THE MAILINGS TAB 8.1

The Mailings Tab 8.3

Printing Envelopes 8.5

Creating a Data Set – Word Document 8.7

Setup Labels 8.9

Lesson Eight Review Questions 8.15

9. FINISH 9.1

Cleanup 9.3

Additional Learning Resources 9.5

A. Glossary of Terms A-1

B. File Management Exercises B-1

C. Notes for Users with Windows XP C-1

D. Index D-1

Introduction

About this book

This book is designed to help you gain skills and confidence in the use of Microsoft Office Word 2007 on a Windows computer. It presents just the basics of a very powerful program, so it is directed at the user new to Word. The book is written for seniors and takes the interests and learning styles of adults into consideration.

You can read this book in a few hours, but that would be a waste of your time. To build your skills for using a comprehensive word authoring program requires practice, dedicated practice, over a period of many days. The book consists of chapters – lessons if you will – that are meant to be studied, practiced, and repeated until you are sure in the concepts and confident in the skills.

You will need more than this book: You need a Windows computer with Microsoft Office Word 2007 installed and equipped with Internet access. It is desirable to have the capability to print out some of your exercises. This book assumes that you have a good working knowledge of the operation of your computer. The main part of the book is written for computers using Windows Vista. If you have installed Word 2007 on a Windows XP machine, you will find specific instructions in the appendix. There are references to those instructions whenever there is a difference between the steps or appearance between Vista and XP.

Each lesson presents a number of related concepts and skills. Succeeding lessons built on the knowledge that you gained in prior chapters. For that reason, you should study this book in the order presented. As you progress, you will often refer back to earlier material – the book intentionally encourages you to repeat skills to strengthen your understanding.

Some of the exercises relate to file management and are not strictly Word skills. These are skills you need to master to use Word effectively so they are included to reinforce your knowledge.

The book uses a number of files to allow you to practice these skills. The files are available on the Internet and there are detailed instructions in the book for downloading and installing these files.

How to use this book

Self-study

You can use this book by yourself, reading and working the exercises. Each lesson covers a number of related skills and concepts and requires a couple of hours to study. After you have completed a lesson, set the book aside. Come back to it the next day; see if you can answer the review questions for the chapter you studied. Use the glossary and index to lead you to understand the material. You will find the illustrations helpful so you know what to expect to see on your computer. You should study the book lesson by lesson as later lessons build on material presented earlier. Once you have finished, you may wish to skip around, reviewing and repeating material as you like.

The book has an extensive index so you may use it as a reference after you have completed your studies. Do use it in that way; being able to find an answer is every bit as good as remembering all the knowledge!

Classroom course manual

This book lends itself to serve as a class manual for an instructor-led course. Normally classroom periods are limited in time. In most situations, your instructor will skip some material in each chapter as there is more material than can be fitted into a two-hour instruction session. Some of the exercises do not lend themselves to classroom work. For example simultaneously downloading material from the Internet would slow down the progress of the class. Your instructor will present alternate methods in class; however, at home as you study and practice,you can do the work as described in the book.

Conventions used in this book

In this manual, most text is in the typeface that you are reading now. Text like this provides information. Some items are set in a different typeface. The references to keys on the keyboard – such as the **Enter** key – are **bolded**. References to controls or buttons you see on the monitor are set in **sans-serif** – such as the **Start** button – so they more closely resemble what you see. Text that you are asked to type verbatim is set in a **mono-spaced** font. When you type the text, it will appear in a different font on the monitor.

Some words are in *italics*. Typically, these are terms that may be unfamiliar to you or that have a specific computer-related meaning. Definitions of these terms will be in the text or in the glossary in the appendix.

Exercises that you do are shown like this so you can find them easily:

Exercise:
* Exercise steps are then described.
* All instructions ar given step by step.
* Each step is marked like this.

Throughout the book you will find the illustrations and the general methods mostly on the left, even numbered, pages and the descriptive text and exercises on the right, odd numbered pages. This layout give you an easy overview of the concepts.

1. Word 2007 Overview

Microsoft Office Word 2007 is a very powerful and capable word processing program. This lesson presents an overview to get you acquainted with its environment.

If you are new to this authoring program, you will learn how to:

- Start the application.
- Understand many of the features of Word.
- Open a document.
- Get around in a document.
- Close the program.

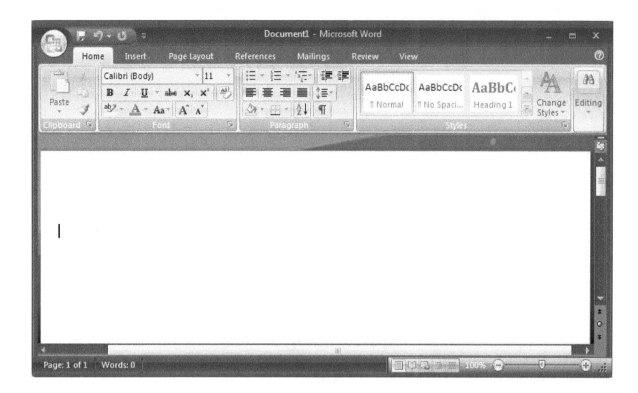

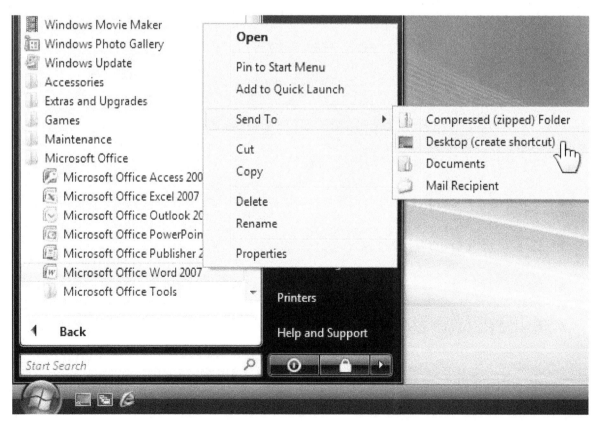

Getting Started

To launch the Word program double-click the Word shortcut icon on the desktop. No shortcut on the desktop? See the box below for instructions.

Exercise:

✱ Double-click the Word shortcut on the desktop.

When Word opens it displays a blank document.

At the top left is the *Office button*. The title bar shows the name of the document as **Document1** followed by **Microsoft Word**. At the right top are the usual Minimize, Maximize, and Close buttons, ⬜⬜❌.

Also on the title bar is the *Quick Access Toolbar*. You use this for often used commands, **Save** 💾, **Undo** ↩, and **Repeat** ↻.

Next from the top is the prominent *Ribbon*. Across the top of the ribbon are tabs which are used to select different parts of the ribbon. The ribbon is divided into groups. When first started, the Home tab is selected. The ribbon displays the many tools and commands so they can be easily found and used.

The illustration on the left shows Word just after it opened. The main area shows the blank document with a lonely cursor blinking at the starting position for text.

There are controls on both sides of the text area and the bottom of the window. You will learn about these in this and other chapters.

Putting a Word shortcut icon on your desktop and the Quick Launch area

See the illustration on the left to guide you.

- Click the **Start** button.
- Click **All Programs.**
- Click **Microsoft Office** – you may have to scroll down.
- Find **Microsoft Office Word 2007** – put the pointer on the entry.
- Right-click – click on **Add to Quick Launch**.
- Right-click on Word again – in the menu find and place the pointer on **Send To**.
- In the next little menu click **Desktop (create shortcut)**.
- Now you have them!

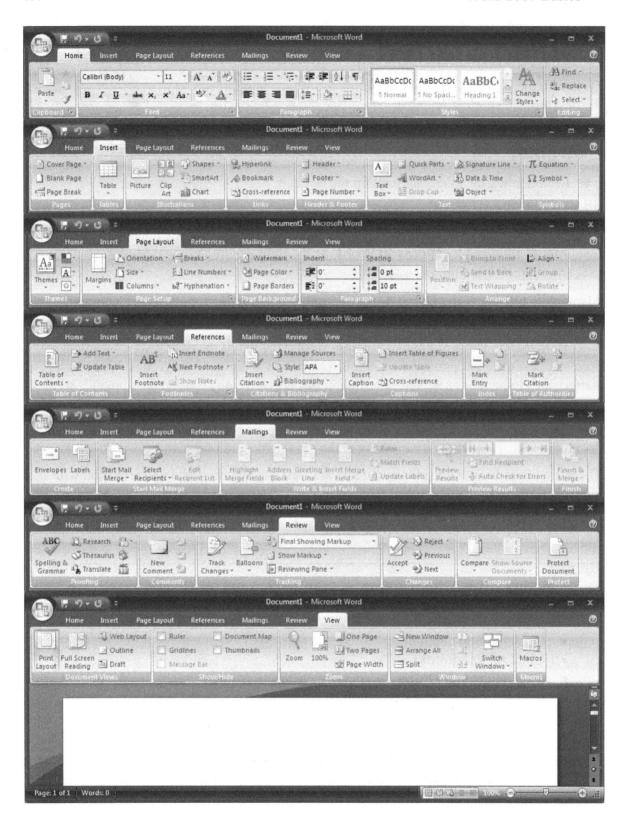

The Ribbon

The *Ribbon* displays the most commonly used commands so you can find them in a glance. It makes your work easy and fast. At the top of the ribbon are seven basic *tabs*. As you click the tabs different portions of the ribbon show commands covered by the subject of the tab. These are called *activity areas*. The basic tabs, shown at the left, are:

- **Home** – with the most commonly used commands for formatting and manipulating text.
- **Insert** – with the commands for doing all the various types of inserting such as pictures, tables, date and time, symbols and many other options.
- **Page Layout** – this portion of the ribbon presents the options for arranging the overall appearance of the document.
- **Reference** – this is where the cross-referencing, indexing and controlling various references is done.
- **Mailings** – with the mail merge commands and the printing of envelopes and labels.
- **Review** – spelling and grammar checking are at home here and some other powerful controls for commenting, tracking, and comparing documents.
- **View** – this is the last basic tab and controls how the document is displayed on the screen.

There are other tabs which are not shown and pop up only when you need them. These will be covered later on.

When Word starts the *Home* tab portion is displayed. In each activity area there are *groups*, sets of related commands, shown in boxes. The group name is shown at the bottom of each box. Many of the commands have little down-pointing arrowheads, ▼, to the right of them. Clicking on that arrowhead displays a *gallery* of the various available options, mostly shown in graphical form.

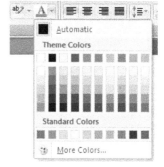

Most group boxes have a little control in the lower right corner called **Dialog Box Launcher** . A click on this control displays a dialog box or task pane with all the options for that group.

Each tab shows the groups related to that tab. Various commands are shown in each group. As you change the width of the Word window the contents of groups may be displayed with more or less information.

Exercise:

❋ Click on tabs, click on the little ▼ arrow heads to display some of the galleries.

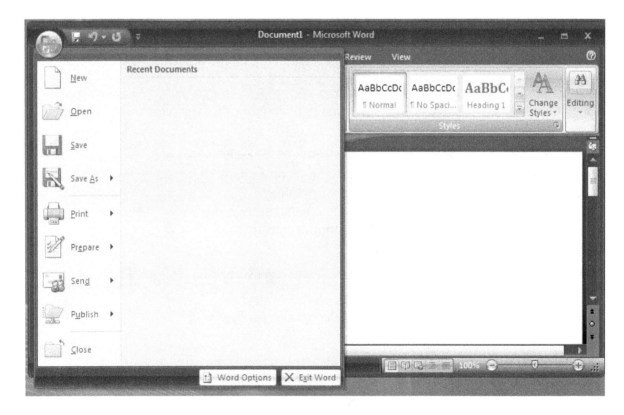

The Office Button

The Office Button is prominent at the upper left corner of the Word window. Like the Start button on the desktop, when you click it a menu is displayed with many commonly used commands. The menu is illustrated at the left. Also like the Start button, there are two panes, the left pane with the commands and the right pane with a listing of recently opened documents. At the start the Recent Documents pane is empty as in the picture on the left.

The commands provided by the Office menu are:

- **New** – for starting a new document. You may not need this since Word starts with a blank document. Clicking the New button presents many templates for different types of documents.

- **Open** – this command is used to open a document, or "load" a document into Word.

- **Save** – the Save command is used to store the document on the hard drive of the computer.

- **Save As** – this button provides a dialog to allow you to specify a document name and a folder name where the document is to be stored.

- **Print** – the Print command sends information to your printer to print the document.

- The **Prepare**, **Send**, and **Publish** commands provide powerful options that will not be covered in this basic course.

- **Close** – the Close button is another way to close Word and functions identically to the Close button in the upper right corner.

Exercise:

* Move the mouse pointer over the **Office** button. Wait for the *Screen Tip* (see top picture on the left).
* Click on the **Office** button.
* Move over the commands on the Office menu. Allow the pointer to rest on some of the commands with right arrow heads, ▶. Inspect the commands in the right pane.

Open a Document

- Click the **Office** button to display the Office menu

- Click the **Open** button

- The Open dialog opens – usually showing the Documents folder. Browse to the location of the file.

- Double-click the file name.

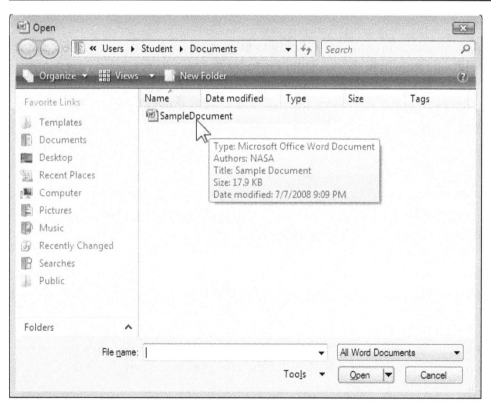

Getting Practice Material

At this point you do not have any of the study files that will help you with the exercises throughout this manual. Before going on, go to page B-3 [XP: C-3] *Download a Sample File from a Website*, and download a sample file from the Senior Academy website.

Opening a Document

 To open, or load, a document, you use the **Open** command located in the Office menu. You reach the Office menu by clicking the Office button in the upper left corner. When you click the **Open** command button the Open dialog is displayed. This is like a "service" of Windows Explorer. You can use all the normal methods for maneuvering, "browsing," in the Open dialog to find the source document.

In the left pane of the Open dialog you select an item, disk or folder, by a single click. The contents of that item is then displayed in the contents pane on the right. To open a folder in the right pane, double-click it.

To open a document when it is displayed in the right, contents, pane, you may double-click it or just click it and then click the **Open** button at the lower right of the Open dialog window.

[XP: C-5]

Exercise:

* ✳ Click the **Office** button.
* ✳ Click the **Open** button.
* ✳ The Open dialog likely shows the contents of your Documents folder. If it does not click **Documents** in the navigation pane on the left.
* ✳ You will see your documents in the contents pane. In the illustration at the left there is only one document in the folder. Double-click **SampleDocument** – or click it (to select it) and click **Open**.

When a document is loaded into Word a copy of the file is put into memory and displayed. This copy may be changed – material changed, added, subtracted – without changing the original file on your hard drive. When you are working in Word you are manipulating the material in memory. This memory is *volatile*, it will be lost when the computer is turned off. Only a *save* operation will write the material to persistent storage on your hard drive. You will learn how to do that later.

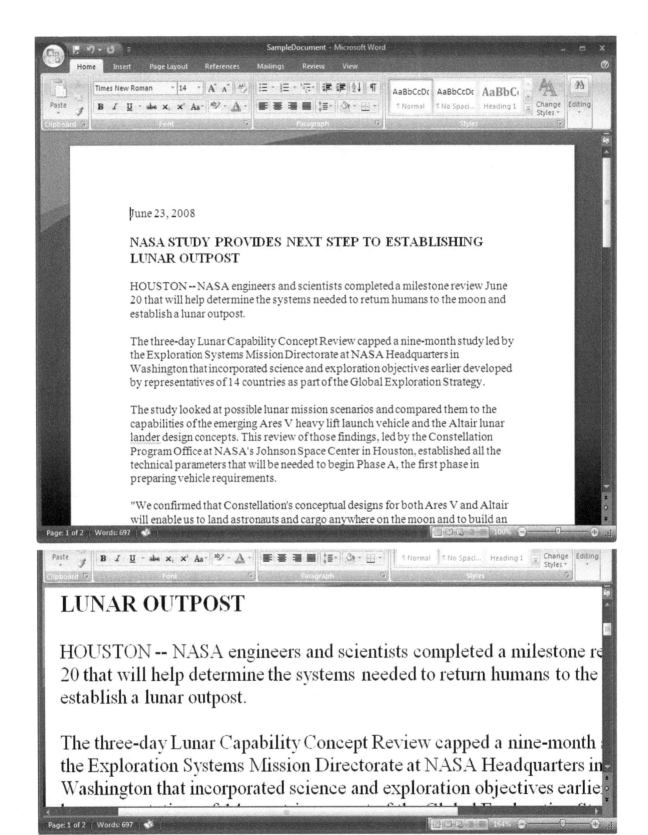

Viewing a Document

When a document is opened it is displayed using the settings that you had when you closed Word the last time. When using Word for the first time the settings are similar to those used for the illustration at the top on the facing page.

You can change the size of the Word window by dragging the borders just as you do with other windows.

Exercise:

❋ Change the size of the Word window by dragging borders or corners.

You can also change the size at which the document is displayed. At the lower right corner of the Word window is the **Zoom** control. This is a slider control for setting the magnification.

Exercise:

❋ Drag the **Zoom** control slider to the left. Notice how the whole document page gets smaller.
❋ Drag the **Zoom** control slider towards the right. Notice how the text gets bigger.
❋ Also notice the horizontal scroll bar appearing and disappearing as you operate the Zoom control.

If the document is long and not all of it can be displayed in the Word window, the portions not displayed can be reached by using the scroll bars.

You can also reach other portions of the document with the **Page Up** and **Page Down** keys. Pressing **Page Down** will move to the next "screen's worth" of text that is farther down in the document. Similarly pressing the **Page Up** key displays text farther up in the document.

If you wish to display the next page, not just the portion that fits in the window, but the text starting at the top of a page, you can use the ⬇ **Next Page** or
⬆ **Previous Page** buttons at the bottom of the vertical scroll bar. See the picture on the right.

Exercise:

❋ Use the **Next Page** button to go to the top of the second page of the document.
❋ Use the **Previous Page** button to go back to the top of the first page.

Navigation keys in text	
← ◄	Moves cursor to left.
→ ►	Moves cursor to right.
↑ ▲	Moves cursor to line above.
↓ ▼	Moves cursor to line below.
Home	Moves cursor to start of line – left margin.
End	Moves cursor to end of line – on right.
Page Down	Moves text and cursor down one "screen's" worth.
Page Up	Moves text and cursor up one "screen's" worth.
Ctrl+PgUp	Moves text and cursor to top of previous page.
Ctrl+PgDn	Moves text and cursor to top of next page.
Ctrl+Home	Moves cursor to start of document.
Ctrl+End	Moves cursor to end of document.

NOTE: When two keys are shown with a plus-sign between, like **Ctrl+End,** that means you hold down the first key while pressing the second key. Pressing a key is pushing it down and immediately letting go.

Moving Around in a Document

On the previous pages you learned how a document is displayed and how to see various portions of a document. That is fine for just reading a document, but if you wish to modify it, or are working on a new document, you need some more precise means of getting around.

In Word, as in any application in which text is entered, there is a _cursor_, also called the _text insertion point_. The cursor is the place where text appears when you type.

When you first open a document the cursor, "text insertion point," will be positioned at the beginning of the document. This is in front of the first character of the document. In the illustrations on the previous pages, the first line is right aligned, so the cursor is in front of the date.

The cursor can be placed anywhere in the document by moving the pointer – note that it will look like an **I** whenever it is over text – to the desired place and clicking.

The navigation keys on the keyboard provide easy controls for moving the cursor around. The table on the left reviews the navigation keys and their functions and specials keys that are commonly used.

Exercise:

* Move the pointer to various places in the text and click to place the cursor.
* Use the arrow keys to move the cursor around in the text.
* Use the **Home** key to place the cursor at the start of the line.
* Use the **End** key to place the cursor at the end of a line of text.
* Use the **Page Down** key to move farther down into the document.
* Use the **Page Up** key to move toward the beginning of the document.
* Use **Ctrl+End** (hold down the **Ctrl** key and press the **End** key) to place the cursor at the end of the document.
* Use **Ctrl+Home** (hold down the **Ctrl** key and press the **Home** key) to place the cursor at the beginning of the document.
* Use **Ctrl+Page Down** to move to the top of the next page.
* Use **Ctrl+Page Up** to move to the top of the previous page (the first page in this case).

* Now close Word by clicking the **Close** button in the top right corner. If the "save reminder" dialog comes up, click the **No** button.

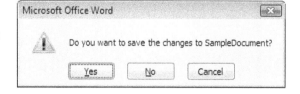

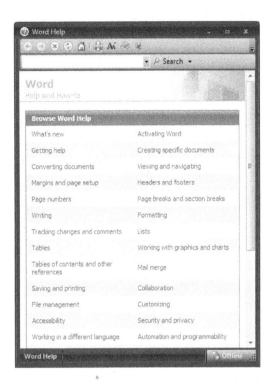

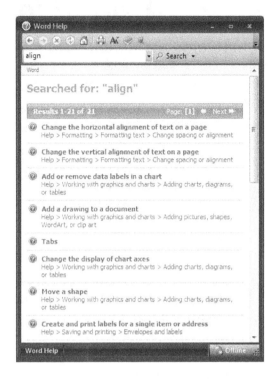

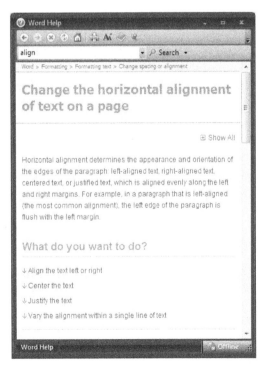

Help

Occasionally you will need some assistance or advice. Word provides comprehensive help.

Near the right top corner there is a small circle with a question mark in it, 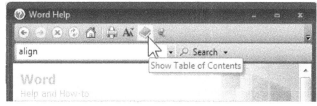, that is the Help button. When you click it, you will see a window similar to the one at left. You may enter a word or phrase in the search box and click the **Search** button.

Exercise:

* ✳ Click the **Help** button.
* ✳ Enter `align` in the search box.
* ✳ Click **Search**.
* ✳ Below **What do you want to do?** Click on **Center the text**.

The illustrations on the left show the successive help windows.

Another way to find the help subject is to click on the **Show Table of Contents** button. The help window now shows the contents of the help system. Clicking on a subject opens a chapter. There may be sub-chapters. Clicking on a subject in the left pane displays the details on the right pane. The picture below shows how it looks. The best way to learn the help system is by trying it out

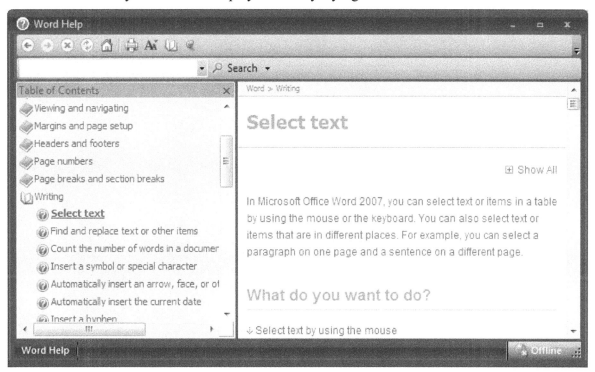

Lesson One Review Questions

A. Where do you find the open command to load a document into Word?

1. It is on the **View** tab.
2. It is on the **Insert** tab.
3. It is on the Office menu that you reach by clicking the **Office** button.

[For answer, see page 1.9]

B. If you click this button , what happens?

1. You temporarily hide the Ribbon so that you have more room for your document.
2. You apply a bigger font size to your text.
3. You see additional options.
4. You add a command to the Quick Access Toolbar.

[For answer, see page 1.5]

C. Where is the Quick Access Toolbar and when should you use it?

1. It is in the upper-left corner of the Word window, and you use it for your frequent commands.
2. It floats above your text, and you use it when you need to make formatting changes.
3. It is in the upper-left corner of the screen, and you should use it when you need to quickly access a document.
4. It is on the **Home** tab, and you should use it when you need to quickly launch or start a new document.

[For answer, see page 1.3]

D. What do you find on a gallery and how do you get to one?

1. A gallery lists all the recently opened documents. It is on the Office menu.
2. The gallery is the funny looking buttons in the **Styles** group on the **Home** tab.
3. A gallery shows options, often in pictorial form. You reach galleries with the down arrow head ▼.
4. You find paintings in a gallery. Ask an artist where to find one.

[For answer, see page 1.5]

Answers: A-3, B-3, C-1, D-3

2. Entering Text

This lesson is about the fundamentals of entering text and managing its appearance. The skills you will learn are ...

- Typing text,
- Specifying fonts and text size,
- Formatting – bold, italic, underline,
- Take advantage of automatic spelling corrections,
- And making bullet or numbered lists.

2.2   Word 2007 Basics

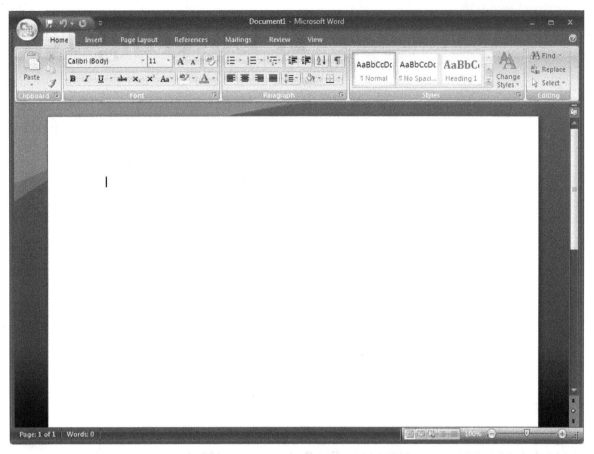

Special keys in text	
Back space	Removes character to *left of the cursor.*
Delete	Removes character to *right of the cursor.*
Enter	Finishes the current paragraph and starts a new one.
Insert	NOT USED – this key is normally disabled in Word.
Shift	When held down yields CAPITAL letters.
Shift	With maneuvering keys: selects (highlights) text.
Caps Lock	Toggles CAPITAL/lower case mode.
Tab	Moves to next tab position (tables, etc.).

Entering Text

Exercise:

✳   Start Word.

When you start Word it comes up with a blank text area. The title bar shows
"Document1 - Microsoft Word." The Home tab is selected and the style is set to Word 2007
Style. The cursor is at the start position and you are ready to enter Normal style text. The font
for Normal style text is Calibri and the font size is set to 11. These defaults can, of course, be
set to your preferences, but for this lesson accept the defaults.

The Home Tab

The Home tab contains the most commonly used commands.

The leftmost group on the **Home** tab is labeled **Clipboard**. This is where you find the **Cut**,
Copy and **Paste** commands.

The next group, **Font**, contains the controls for managing the appearance of text such as
setting the font, size, and other aspects.

The **Paragraph** group is next with the common commands for formatting text on the
paragraph level.

The **Styles** group offers the very powerful and convenient Styles options.

The **Editing** group includes the Find and Replace commands.

In this lesson you will use the first three groups.

Special Keys

Note the table at the left. A number of special keys and their functions are explained in the
table. You will be using these keys often.

Components of a Document

Text consists, of course, of letters, numbers, and symbols. Words are made of these
characters and separated from each other by spaces and punctuation marks. Words in turn
form sentences. Sentences may be combined into paragraphs. The whole document consists
of these parts. In word processing these parts can be manipulated in many ways. Word
processors need to know the boundaries of these parts. Spaces and punctuation marks are
used to identify words and sentences. Paragraphs are identified with the **Enter** key. The
Enter key is only used to end a paragraph. It is not needed at the end of a line. "Word-
wrapping" automatically puts words on the next line when there is insufficient room at the
end of the line.

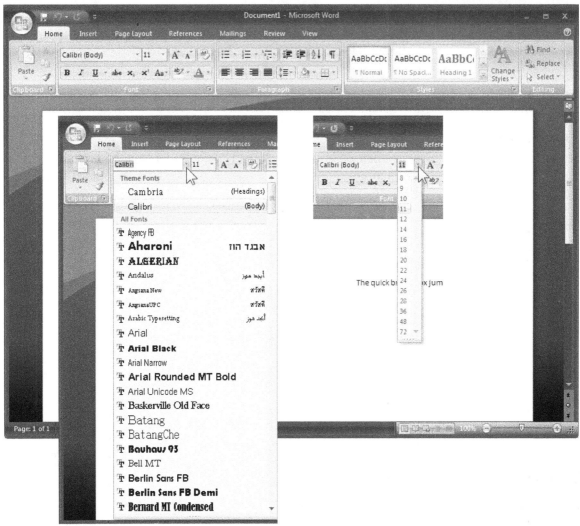

Selecting Font and Size

•	On the **Home** tab in the **Font** group click on ▼ to the right of the font box.
•	Click on the font name to select it. Scroll down if needed.
•	Click on the ▼ to the right of the size box.
•	Click on the desired size.

Typing Text

Exercise:

* With Word open and a blank document displayed, type the following text: **The quick brown fox jumped over the lazy dogs.**
* Press the **Return** key to end the paragraph.

This sentence is often used in typing exercises because it contains all the letters of the alphabet.

You can specify how text will appear by setting the formatting in the Font group on the Home tab. Some exercises will make that clear.

Font and Size

Font, the shape of the characters and the size are selected in the **Font** group. A large number of fonts are installed on your computer. Clicking on the ▼ next to the font name box displays a long list of font names, so long that you need the scroll bar to get to them all. The font list shows some "theme" fonts at the top, then recently used fonts, and then an alphabetic listing by font name.

Similarly, the size is selected by clicking the ▼ next to the size box. You can also type the desired size into the size box. In addition there are a couple of commands to increase the size, A, and to decrease the size, A.

Exercise:

* Click on the ▼ next to the box with the name of the current font. Scroll down to find **Times New Roman** in the listing and click on it.
* Click on the size selector arrow and click on **28**.
* Now type: **The quick brown fox**. Notice the different font and size.
* Select **Brush Script** font and size **36**.
* Type: **jumped over the lazy dogs**. The text should appear similar to the illustration below. Note that you may get word wrapping as shown here.
* Try some other fonts and sizes.

The quick brown fox jumped over the lazy dogs.

The quick brown fox *jumped over the lazy dogs.*

Formatting Text

Besides font and size there are other formatting you can apply to text. The Font box also shows these commands:

Bold

The **Bold** command, **B** , allows you to type **bold** text. Click on the control to engage bold type – note how the command button changes color – click it again to disengage bold mode.

Italic

The **Italic** command, *I* , allows you to type *italic, leaning*, text. It toggles its function like the bold command.

Underline

The Underline command, **U** , provides for underlined text. It turns on and off by clicking like the other commands in this group. There is a control to select the type of underline. See the illustration on the left.

Other Formatting Options

Other commands allow ~~strikethrough~~ of text, offer subscripting as in H_2O, superscripting like in $E=mc^2$. Try these yourself.

Exercise:

* ❋ Select **Times New Roman** font.
* ❋ Set the size to **24**
* ❋ Now click on the **Bold** command.
* ❋ Type some text.
* ❋ Click on the **Italic** command.
* ❋ Type some more text.
* ❋ Click the **Underline** command.
* ❋ Type some more text.
* ❋ Click **Bold** again to release bolding, and type additional text.
* ❋ Try various combinations to learn how the commands all work.
* ❋ Close Word. Click **No** when it asks about saving.

Correcting Text	
Backspace	Use **Backspace** to erase a character ahead, to the left, of the cursor.
Delete	Use **Delete** to erase a character behind, to the right of, the cursor.

The quaack brom|

The qua|ck brown

Correcting Text

As you type you may find that you hit the wrong key or you changed your mind about what you just typed. If it is just the last few characters, the easiest way to undo what you just typed is to use the **Backspace** key. The **Backspace** key "erases" the character immediately to the left of the cursor.

To erase a character to the right of the cursor, you use the **Delete** key.

In the following exercise you can practice correcting text. First change the font and size of the text. Notice when changing the font that the font gallery now has a new section near the top with the most recently used fonts.

As you type the incorrect text in the exercise, ignore the wavy underlines. These indicate errors in spelling or grammar. A later lesson will cover that topic.

Exercise:

* Set the font to **Times New Roman** and the size to **18**.
* Type **The quaack brom**
* Use the **Backspace** key to erase the "**m**" and type **wn** to make the correction.
* Move the pointer to between the a's and click. The cursor will now be at that position.
* Press the **Backspace** key to erase the **a** to the left of the cursor.
* Press the **Delete** key to erase the **a** to the right of the cursor.
* Type **i** to correct the word.
* Press the **End** key to return to the end of the line.
* Continue making errors and correcting them.
* Press the **Enter** key a couple of times.
* Now set the font size to **36** for the next exercise.

AutoCorrect - Defaults
• First letter in a sentence is automatically capitalized.
• Double capital letters are corrected – **THe** becomes **The**.
• Caps Lock is automatically turned off when typing the first letter of a word with Shift held down.
• Many incorrectly typed words are automatically corrected.

The quick Brown Fox jUMPED

The quick Brown Fox Jumped |

Cancel AutoCorrect Action
• After the unwanted correction: Type **Ctrl-Z**
• Alternate method: Click the **Undo** icon 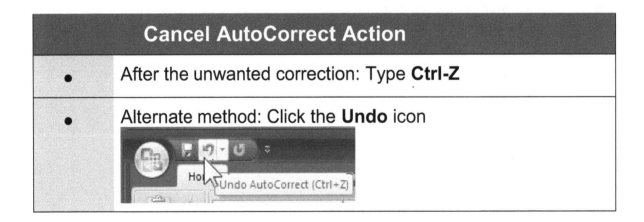

AutoCorrect – The Automatic Helper

There is more to entering text than you might expect. Word has a built in helper called *AutoCorrect*. This feature is turned on by default and you will want to keep it that way. Here a number of the AutoCorrect features are discussed.

It is normal to capitalize the first letter in a new sentence or paragraph. Word will do that automatically for you. If you accidentally hold down the Shift key too long and type a couple of capital letters at the beginning of a word, Word will correct that also. If you accidentally leave the **Caps Lock** on and type a word that should be capitalized (by holding down the Shift key for the first letter), Word will make the correction and release the Caps Lock.

Try these features in the following exercise. Be sure to make the errors as specified.

Exercise:

* If you have not already done so, set the font to **Times New Roman** and the size to **36**.
* Type the following: **the quick**

Notice how the word **the** is changed to **The** the moment you type the space after the word.

* Type the following: **BRown fox**

Notice how **BRown** was changed to **Brown** when you typed the space after the word.

* Press the **Caps Lock** key to turn capitalization on.
* Hold down the **Shift** key and type the letter **J**.
* Release the **Shift** key and type **umped**
* Don't type the space just yet so you can inspect the result. It should look like this: **jUMPED**
* Now type the space and notice the change.

There is more. Word will also automatically correct a large number of typographical errors. The following exercise illustrates a number of these.

* Now type **ovre**. Type the following space – the word will change to **over**.
* Now type **teh**.
* Now type **lazy doggs**.
* Press **Enter** to start a new paragraph.

Notice how the words *over*, *the*, and *dogs* were automatically corrected.

What if you don't want the correction? You might want to intentionally show mistyped words, like on this page. To cancel the AutoCorrect action – as soon as the correction appears (after you type the space), hold down the **Ctrl** key and press the **Z** key or click the **Undo** icon.

This way ➔ in. Hello ☺. Don't
be ☹. Have a smile as your ™
trademark. You can © it. Who
was 1ˢᵗ, 2ⁿᵈ, 3ʳᵈ, and 4ᵗʰ?|

Here we "quote text" – this is
an n-dash—this is an m-dash.

Use ½ cup milk, ¼ stick butter,
1/3 cup cocoa, ⅓ cup raisins.|

To find the AutoCorrect options:

Click the **Office Button.**

Click [Word Options] (at the bottom).

Click [Proofing]

The AutoCorrect window lets you set
preferences and shows the "replace
with" table – a very long table, you will
have to scroll a long way to see them all.
You can add your own replace-with
options in this dialog.

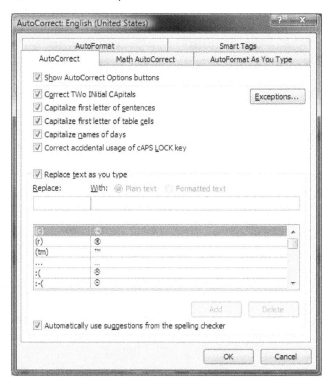

More AutoCorrect Features

AutoCorrect also lets you enter a number of symbols by just typing specific text. Here are a few of these.

Exercise:

* Type **This ==> way in. Hello :). Don't be :(. Have a smile as your (tm) trademark. you can (c) it. who was 1st, 2nd, 3rd, and 4th?**

See the illustration on the left for the results.

Word will use the proper quote marks and insert n-dashes and m-dashes where appropriate. Here is an illustration of that:

Exercise:

* Press **Enter** to start a new paragraph.
* Type: **Here we "quote text" - this is an n-dash--this is an m-dash.**

To make a n-dash, you type *space, hyphen, space*.

To make an m-dash type *hyphen, hyphen* without leading or trailing spaces.

A couple more:

Exercise:

* Press **Enter** to start a new paragraph.
* Type: **use 1/2 cup milk, 1/4 stick butter, 1/3 cup cocoa,**

Note that 1/3 did not change. How can you get that?

* Click the Superscript command x^2 .
* Type: **1**
* Click the Superscript command x^2 – to clear it.
* Type **/**
* Click the Subscript command . x_2
* Type: **3**
* Click the Subscript command x_2 – to clear it.
* Type: **cup raisins**.

Note that the size of the $^1/_3$ does not quite match – for now that is close enough.

- Milk
- Butter
- Cocoa
- Raisins

1. Milk
2. Butter
3. Cocoa
4. Raisins

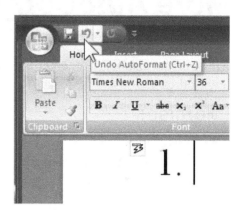

AutoFormat - Defaults
• Start a new paragraph with an asterisk, *, and a space to get a bullet list.
• Start a new paragraph with a number, . (period), and space to get a numbered list – 1.　　2.　　….
• Start a new paragraph with a number,), and space to get a numbered list – 1)　　2)　　….

Cancel AutoFormat Action
• After the unwanted formatting: Type **Ctrl-Z**.
• Alternate method: Click the **Undo** icon.

Automatic Bullets and Numbered Lists

Sometimes you would like to show a list of items as shown on the left. In another lesson you will learn about lists, but here you see the quick way. It is covered here because you might get these "features" when you don't expect them.

Word has a feature called *AutoFormat*. To start a bullet list type an *asterisk*, a *space*, and then your text. After you press the **Enter** key, the next bullet will already be shown. To stop the list press the **Enter** key once more.

Exercise:

* Press the **Enter** key to start a new paragraph.
* Type: `* milk`
* Press the **Enter** key
* Type: `butter`
* Press **Enter**, type: `cocoa`
* Press **Enter**, type `raisins`
* Press **Enter**.
* Press **Enter**.

Notice how the list is nicely bulleted and the words are automatically capitalized.

Now for a numbered list. To start an automatically numbered list you start a line with the first number followed by a *period* or an *open-parenthesis* mark, a *space*, and then your text.

Exercise:

* Press the **Enter** key to start a new paragraph.
* Type: `1. milk`
* Press the **Enter** key
* Type: `butter`
* Press **Enter**, type: `cocoa`
* Press **Enter**, type `raisins`
* Press **Enter**.
* Press **Enter**.

How do you prevent the bulleting or numbering from starting automatically?

The **Undo** command or **Ctrl-Z** will allow you to place the asterisk or number without engaging the list feature.

Lesson Two Review Questions

A. When entering text near the right margin how do you start a new line?

1. You press the **Tab** key.
2. You press the **Enter** key.
3. You just keep typing.

[For answer, see page 2.3]

B. When you want a numbered list what do you do?

1. You type the number then press the **Tab** key and then type.
2. You type the number a period a space and then your text.
3. You click on the **Numbering** command and then type your text.
4. Any of the above.

[For answer, see page 2.15]

C. How do you make a copyright symbol?

1. You press the **Alt** key and type the letter c.
2. You type "(c)".
3. You type "circle-c".

[For answer, see page 2.13]

D. When you want to start a line with an *asterisk* what do you do?

1. You type two asterisks press **Backspace** and go on.
2. You type an asterisk a space then **Ctrl-Z** and go on.
3. You type a space an asterisk another space and go on.

[For answer, see page 2.15]

E. Where do you find the underline control?

1. On the **Insert** tab in the **Text** group.
2. On the **Home** tab in the **Font** group.
3. In the lower right corner of the Word window.
4. It is on the **Home** tab, and you should use it when you need to quickly launch or start a new document.

[For answer, see page 2.7

Answers: A-3, B-4, C-2, D-2, E-2

3. Creating, Saving and Managing Files

Making documents is all about having the use of them at a later time and being able to share them. So creating, saving, and managing documents is an integral part of using an authoring program.

This lesson is a little about Word and a lot about file management. If you are skilled in the use of your computer, some of the material will be quite familiar. If you are a relatively new user, you may gain many skills in this lesson.

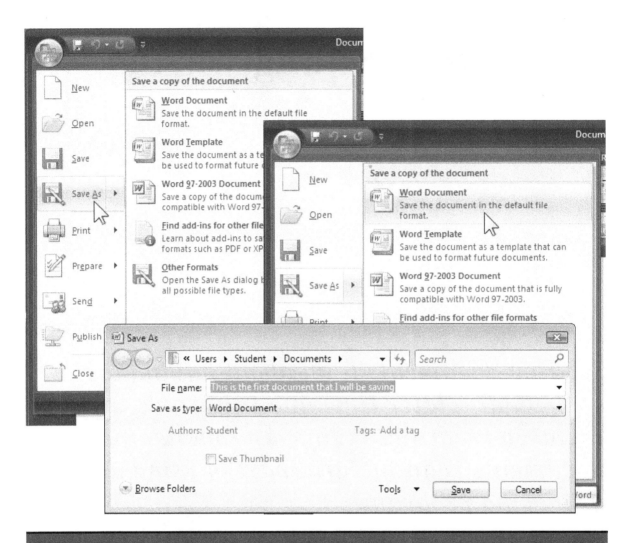

Save a Document – in Documents

- Click **Office** button to open the Office menu.

- Click **Save As**.

- Enter name of document in Save As dialog.

- Click **Save**.

Creating a Document

When you first enter text into a blank document – it shows **Document1** in the title bar – the information resides in the computers operating memory. It will be lost when Word is closed or power is lost if it is not written to persistent storage such as your hard drive or attached storage like a flash drive.

If you want to keep the document for future use, you must *save* it. There are several ways to save, here you will use the most "formal" method.

[XP: C-7]

Exercise:

* Start Word.
* Enter some text. If you don't know what to type, here is a suggestion: **This is the first document that I will be saving**.
* Click the **Office** button,
* Move the pointer down to the **Save As** command. It will change color and a menu will appear in the right pane.
* Click **Word Document** in the right pane.

This will bring up the Save As dialog. It will look similar to the picture on the left.

At the top is the address bar, this is where you specify the storage location for the document. By default it will show the Documents folder address. This is where you will store most of your documents. When you have many documents, you will want to store them in a folder, or a sub-folder, within the Documents folder. You will learn more about that shortly. For now, the Documents folder is the right place. In the bottom pane is the **File name:** box. This is a text entry box where you specify the name for the document. Word uses part of the first line of the document as the default name. You can overtype it. Here just accept the default name.

There is a Save as type: control. Accept the default Word Document setting.

Exercise:

* Click the **Save** command in the **Save As** dialog window.
* Close Word. It will close without asking to confirm saving because you just did.

You have created a document. It is stored in the Documents folder. Its name is **This is the first document that I will be saving**. Yes, all of that is the document's name.

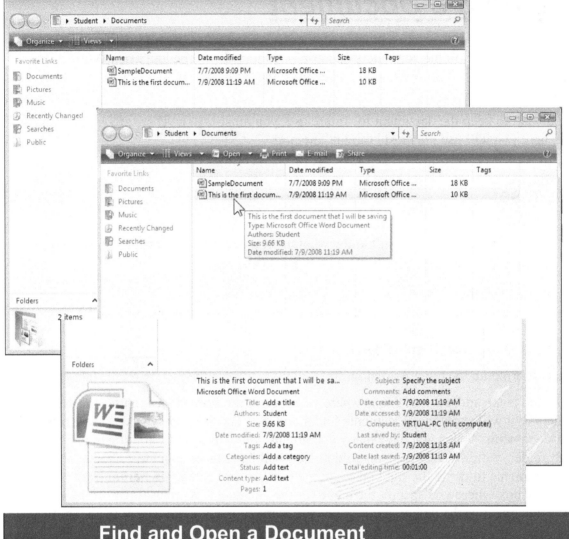

Find and Open a Document

•	Click **Start**.
•	Click **Documents**.
•	Find the document – scroll and browse.
•	Double-click on the document listing (icon or name).

Finding a Saved Document

Did you really just save a document? Open it back up as described in the following exercise.

[XP: C-9]

Exercise:

* Click **Start**.
* Click **Documents**.

Windows Explorer opens showing the contents of the Documents folder. On your computer at home there may be many other items in this folder. Here there is just the file you downloaded from the Internet earlier and the newly created file. Notice that most likely not all of the name will show. This is one of the reasons why it is good to give documents short names.

Exercise:

* Click on the name of the document you created.

Notice that detailed information is shown in the details pane at the bottom.

No details pane? Click **Organize**, move the pointer down to **Layout**, in the little menu click **Details Pane**. You can drag the top border of the details pane to change its size. This also varies the amount of information that is shown.

Notice that the text of the document is displayed in the preview pane and all sorts of details are listed in the details pane.

Exercise:

* Double-click on the document name. Word opens showing the document.

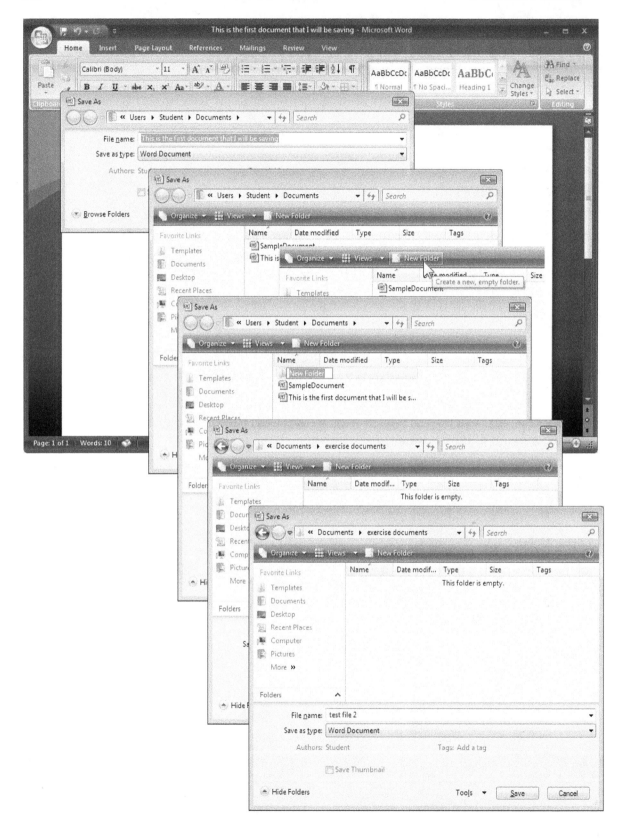

Saving as a New Document

Notice that the newly opened document now has its name shown on the title bar. Go ahead and add some additional text.

Exercise:

> ✳ Add some text to the document. This will do: **Here is some additional text**.

Now you will save the document in its new form, but without overwriting the first document. In fact you will store it in a newly created folder inside the Documents folder.

[XP: C-11]

Exercise:

> ✳ Start the save process as before: Click the **Office** button, click **Save As** (You don't really have to click on Word Document, this is the default.)
> ✳ Click **Browse Folders**.

This enlarges the Save As dialog. It now looks similar to Windows Explorer because it is Windows Explorer, just with a different "hat" on.

Create a New Folder

In the Save As dialog there is a command to create a new folder. This works exactly the same way that it works in the normal Windows Explorer window.

Exercise:

> ✳ Click **New Folder** on the tool bar in the Save As dialog window.
> ✳ The new folder is shown in the contents pane. Note that the name is in a box, a text entry box!, and is selected so you can just type over it. Enter the name of the new folder. Use: **exercise documents**.
> ✳ Press **Enter**.
> ✳ The contents of the new folder will be shown; it is empty, of course.
> ✳ Click in the File name: box. The name will be selected so you can just type in the new name. Use: **test file 2**.
> ✳ Click **Save**.

The file is saved. Notice that the Word window title bar now shows the new name.

Exercise:

> ✳ Close Word.

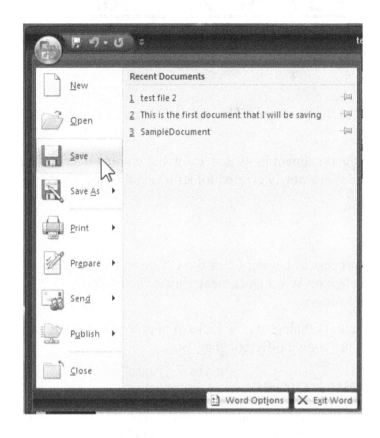

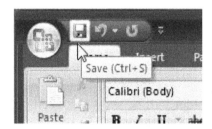

The Save Command

You have learned to save a document using the **Save As** command. There is also a **Save** command available in a couple of locations. It is very important for you to know the difference between these commands and when to use them.

When you open or load a document into Word, the information in the file on your computer drive is copied into the working memory of the machine. It is this copy that is displayed in Word and that you can modify, add to, delete from, and otherwise manipulate.

The **Save As** command allows you to store a new file with the modified information in Word on your computer. You have encountered and used this command already.

The **Save** command is different. It replaces the stored file with the material currently in the Word program – and thus in the working memory. The previous file is overwritten and thus destroyed. **Word does not ask for permission to destroy the old file!**

So is **Save** a dangerous command? Indeed it is! So why is it there? Because it is also an extremely useful command.

As you are working on a document, say a letter, you add some text, think about it, and add some more text. It takes a while to prepare a document, it is not just the typing time, but also the time to contemplate and organize your thoughts. What **Save** is good for is to allow you to save the document periodically. You can save, take a break, and come back to your work. Should the power have gone out, or your pet unplugged the computer, the document in memory is lost. You can recover the last stored version. So clicking **Save** frequently is a good way to assure peace of mind and safeguard your work.

Remember, however, whenever you click **Save**, the previously stored file is replaced. If you just deleted a section of text, click **Save**, and then change your mind about the deletion, you are in trouble. Even though your computer may have a microphone, swearing at it will not recover the material. So use **Save As** for safekeeping of a document version that you might want to come back to. Use **Save** as you add material so you will not lose the latest additions.

The **Save** command is located in the Office menu, you reach it by clicking the **Office Button**.

The **Save** command, 🖫 , is also found in the **Quick Access Toolbar** – normally at the top left of the Word window (see picture at left).

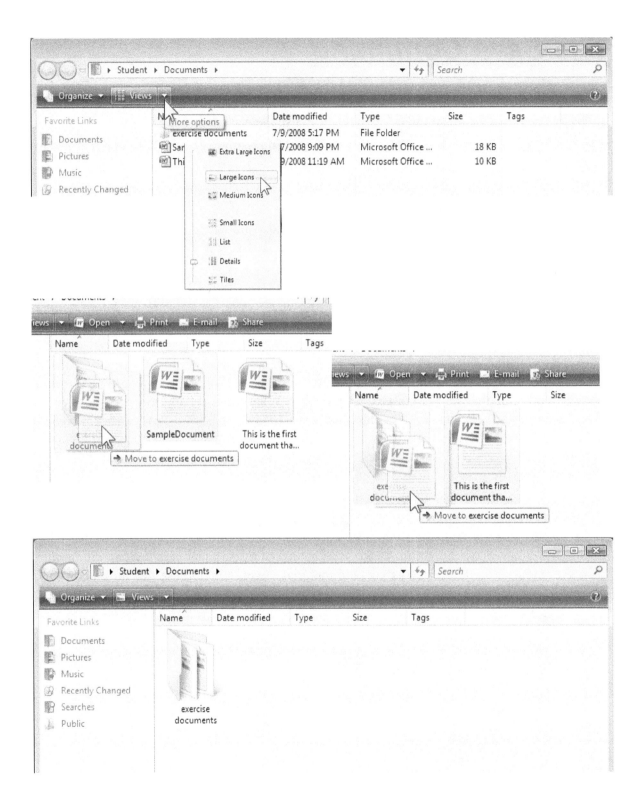

Moving Files

Organizing files by creating folders, moving the files and naming them in a meaningful manner may not seem like a true part of learning Word; however, the exercises in this lesson present important skills. If you know this material well you will find this an easy lesson.

In the following exercise you will move a file by dragging it to its destination folder. When dragging files within a drive (such as the C: drive), that is, from one location on the drive, to another location on the same drive, files are moved. Moving a file means that it is removed from the source location and placed into the destination location.

You will now move the file you downloaded from the Internet and the first file that you created from the Documents folder to the exercise documents folder that you made within the Documents folder.

Exercise:

* ✳ Click **Start**.
* ✳ Click **Documents**.
* ✳ Change the view of the contents pane to large icons. Click the ▼ next to **View**, then click **Large Icons**.
* ✳ Find the file **SampleDocument** and drag it to the **exercise documents** folder.
* ✳ Find the file **This is the first ...** and drag it to the **exercise documents** folder.
* ✳ Drag it to the **exercise documents** folder.

Why did you change the view to large icons? Because large items are easier to drag and the large folder icon presents a larger "target"!

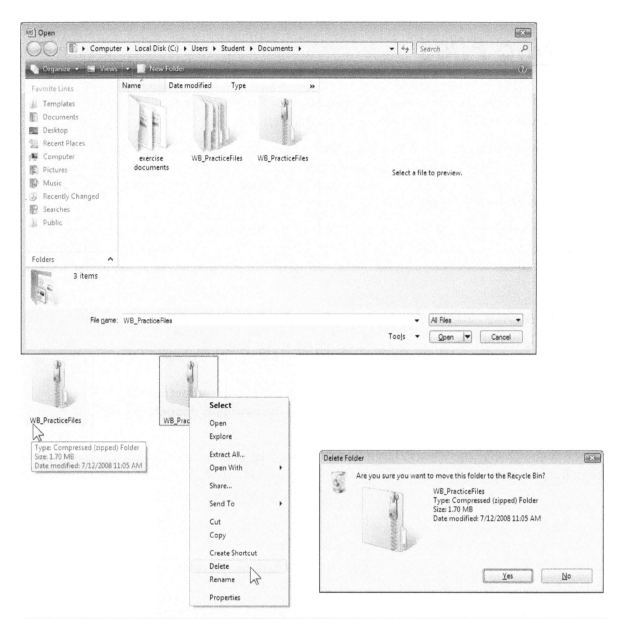

Delete a File or Folder

•	Right-click the item name or icon.
•	Click **Delete** in the drop-down menu.
•	Click **Yes** in the Delete File or Delete Folder dialog.

Organizing Files and Folders

For the next exercises, you will need more files to work with. Download practice files from the Senior Academy website as described in *Download a Compressed File from a Website* on page B-5 [XP: C-15]. Then extract the contents from the file, see *Expand a Compressed File* on page B-7 [XP: C-17].

In the following exercises you will learn how the Open dialog can be used just like Windows Explorer to manage your files.

The files you downloaded are poorly organized. This is intentional, of course, just to give you the opportunity to practice file management skills.

If you are using Windows XP please turn to page C-19 for the exercises.

Exercise:

* Open Word. You may do so by clicking the Word icon in the Quick Launch area of the taskbar or by double-clicking the Word shortcut on the Desktop.
* Click the **Office Button**.
* Click **Open**.

The Open dialog should resemble the illustration at the left. If you do not have the Preview pane open, open it by clicking **Organize – Layout**, then in the little menu click **Preview Pane**. On your own computer you will also see your other files. Here we are concerned only with the ones shown in the illustration.

Deleting a File or Folder

You no longer need the file you downloaded from the Senior Academy website since you have extracted its contents. This file is called WB_PracticeFiles.zip, the extension may not be shown, but you can recognize it by the zipper.

[XP: C-19]

Exercise:

* Hover the pointer on the **WB_PracticeFiles** icon with the zipper. Note that it is described as a "Compressed (zipped) Folder".
* Right-click on the icon or name.
* In the drop-down menu click **Delete**.
* In the Delete Folder dialog click **Yes** to move the file to the Recycle Bin.

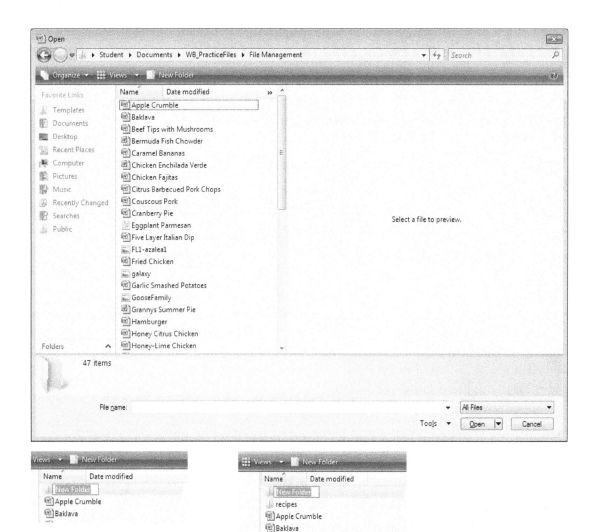

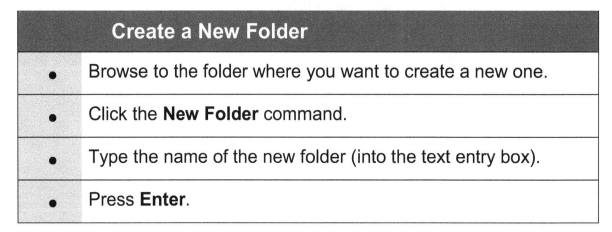

Create a New Folder

•	Browse to the folder where you want to create a new one.
•	Click the **New Folder** command.
•	Type the name of the new folder (into the text entry box).
•	Press **Enter**.

Creating a New Folder

Still using the Open dialog to practice file management, you will now move around in the practice files folder and create a couple of new folders. The folder File Management contains 47 items; some are pictures, some are recipes. These files clearly are not well organized. For the next exercise, you will create two new folders and move the files into the appropriate new folder.

[XP: C-21]

Exercise:

* Double-click the **WB_PacticeFiles** icon or name. The contents of the folder is now displayed in the contents pane.
* Double-click the **File Management** folder to display the contents of that folder.

* Click the arrow, ▼, next to the **View** command and select **Small Icons** (this may already be the view). The Open dialog should now resemble the illustration at the left.
* Click **New Folder**. A new folder is added in the contents pane. The folder name is selected in a text entry box so you can just type the name of the new folder.
* Type: **recipes** as the name of the new folder.
* Press **Enter**.
* Click **New Folder** to create another folder.
* Type: **pictures** as the name of this new folder.
* Press **Enter**.

You now have two new folders to allow you to re-organize the files in this folder.

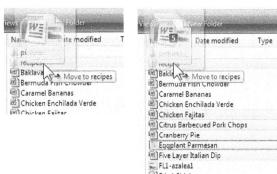

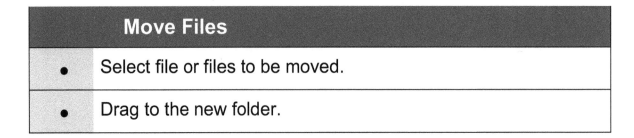

Move Files

•	Select file or files to be moved.
•	Drag to the new folder.

Moving Files

To organize the files in this folder, move the each file into the "recipe" folder if it is a recipe, into the "pictures" folder if it is a picture. For this exercise the Preview pane is used to allow you to identify the type of file you are dealing with.

NOTE: For this exercise you should have opened Word and launched the Open dialog. In the dialog you should have browsed to the File Management folder in WB_PraticeFiles. The Preview pane should be open and the File Types set to All Files. (See illustration at left.)

[XP: C-23]

Exercise:

* Click on a file. Note that the Preview pane shows the contents of the file.
* Drag the file to the appropriate folder. Note that when the pointer is over the folder there is a screen tip showing "**move to ...**" with the folder name. This helps you to move the file to the correct folder. When you are on the correct folder, release the mouse button. The file will be moved.
* Repeat this several times more, dragging recipe files to the recipe folder and picture files to the picture folder.
* Identify several recipe files. Select these files by holding down the **Ctrl** key and click the files.
* Now place the pointer on any of the selected files and drag them (press the left mouse button) to the recipe folder. Note how the number of files is shown.
* Continue until all files have been moved.

When you are finished check your work. You should have 10 pictures in the pictures folder. The other 37 files are recipe documents and should now be in the recipe folder.

Lesson Three Review Questions

A. What happens when you drag a folder from one location to another?

1. It is moved, regardless of location or drive.
2. It is always copied to the new location.
3. It is copied when you drag from a location on one drive to a location on another drive. It is moved when you drag from one location to another on the same drive.
4. Nothing happens.

[For answer, see page **Error! Bookmark not defined.**]

B. Where do you find the Save As command?

1. On the **Home** tab in the **Editing** group.
2. On the **Insert** tab in the **Links** group.
3. In the **Office** menu.
4. In the **Start** menu.

[For answer, see page 3.7]

C. Where do you find the New Folder command?

1. On the **Insert** tab in the **Links** group.
2. In the **Office** menu under **New**.
3. In the **Windows Explorer** under **Organize**.
4. On the tool bar In the **Save As** dialog

[For answer, see page 3.7 or 3.15]

D. What does the Save command do?

1. It creates a new file and allows you to give it a new name.
2. It replaces the file on the disk with the modified document displayed on the screen.
3. It stores an additional file by the same name alongside the old one.

[For answers see page 3.9]

Answers: A-3, B-3, C-3 and 4 – trick question!, D-2.

4. Modifying Text

The formatting of entered text is not irredeemably fixed. Text can be modified at any time.

In this lesson you will learn how to ...

- *Select text – word, line, sentence, paragraph, range of words, range of text,*
- *Format selected text, bold, italic, color and more,*
- *Cut, copy, and paste text,*
- *Move text around,*
- *Align the text, left, center, right, and justified.*

"text entry" point|← Cursor
I← Pointer

Cursor and Pointers in Word window
• Cursor – a blinking vertical bar – shows the text entry point
• Pointer – in text area an I-beam shape – click anywhere in text to place cursor – drag over text to select
• Pointer – left of text – arrow shape – click to select line – double-click to select paragraph – Triple-click to select the entire document
• Pointer – elsewhere – normal pointer shape

In this sentence, this text has been selected.

This lesson will present the real power of word processing: manipulating text with ease. First another bit of review:

Cursor and Pointer

In a Word window there is a *pointer* and a *cursor*. The cursor is at the "text entry point" and that is the formal name of the cursor. The mouse pointer takes on several shapes. When over text it is the shape of the capital letter I. In the left margin it is an arrow pointing toward upper right. Elsewhere it is the normal arrow pointing toward upper left. The illustration and table on the left provide a reference for you.

When a document is first opened the cursor will be positioned at the start of the document. That is in front of the first character in the document. In Lesson One you learned how to navigate around in a document.

Placing and Moving the Cursor

You already learned how to place the cursor anywhere in the text: Move the pointer to the desired location and click. You also learned that the curser can be moved with the navigation keys: the arrow keys, ▲, ▼, ◄, ►, **Page Up** and **Page Down**, the **Home** and **End** keys, and several key combinations. If you need a refresher review page 1.13.

Text is *selected* so you can do something with it. Selecting text is a way to tell the Word program what part of the text you want to take some action on. There are many things you can do with text, but first it must be selected. When text is selected it appears as if a blue highlighter had been brushed over it.

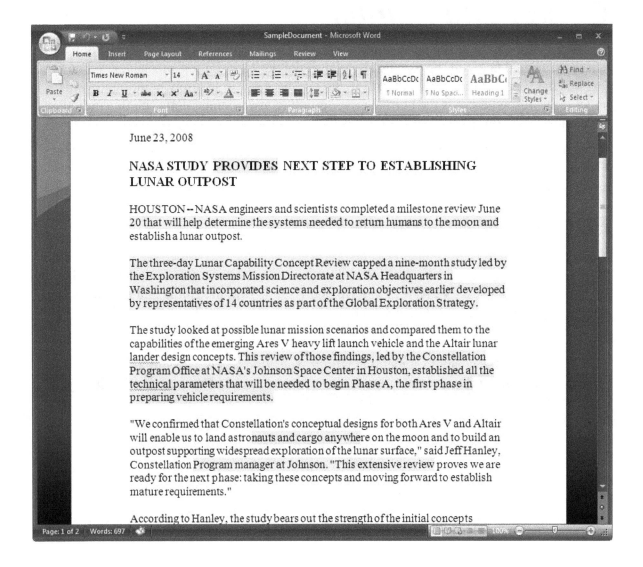

Selecting Text

Here are different ways to select text:

Select a Word

Double-click on a word to select it.

Select a Line

Move the pointer into the left margin in front of the line – so that the pointer turns into an arrow. Now click – the line is selected.

Select a Paragraph

Move the pointer into the left margin in front of the paragraph – so that the pointer turns into an arrow. Now double-click – the paragraph is selected.

Select a Sentence

Hold down the **Ctrl** key and click anywhere in the sentence.

Select a Range of Characters or Words

Click at the beginning point to place the cursor. Hold down the **Shift** key and press the right (or other) arrow key until the cursor is at the end point of the selection range.

Select a Range of Text

With the pointer at the start of the range of text press down the left mouse button, drag to the end point and release the mouse button. Note: There is a setting in Word to make this action select whole words only. This is the default setting.

The illustration on the left shows an example of each type of these selections. There are numerous other ways of selecting text, but these should suffice for now.

"Unselect" a selection

To cancel a selection, click anywhere inside or outside the selected text.

Exercise:

* Open a document: Click **Start** – click **Documents** – double-click **WB_PracticeFiles** – double-click **SampleDocument**.
* Practice selecting words, lines, paragraphs, sentences, and ranges of text and words.

So what can you do with selected text? Many things – as you will learn next!

June 23, 2008

NASA STUDY PROVIDES NEXT STEP TO ESTABLISHING LUNAR OUTPOST

June 23, 2008

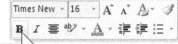

NASA STUDY PROVIDES NEXT STEP TO ESTABLISHING LUNAR OUTPOST

June 23, 2008

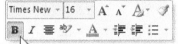

NASA STUDY PROVIDES NEXT STEP TO ESTABLISHING LUNAR OUTPOST

June 23, 2008

NASA STUDY PROVIDES NEX LUNAR OUTPOST

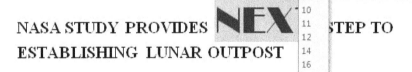

HOUSTON -- NASA engineers and sc   June
20 that will help determine the systems   and
establish a lunar outpost.

June 23, 2008

NASA STUDY PROVIDES NEX STEP TO ESTABLISHING LUNAR OUTPOST

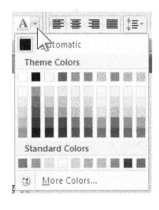

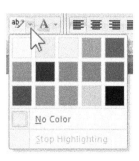

The Mini Toolbar

As you may have discovered as you were practicing selecting text, there is a feature in Word called the Mini Toolbar. It pops up whenever some text is selected. It then provides the most common commands for modifying the text. Take a look.

Exercise:

✳ Select the word "NEXT" in the first line of the document title. Notice that the pointer changes from the I-beam to the normal pointer and a faint outline of the Mini Toolbar appears. See illustrations at left.
✳ Move the pointer over the Mini Toolbar and it will "darken" to a normal view. Note that the Bold command is "on" (colored and boxed) – the text you selected is already bold.
✳ Click on the **Bold** command in the Mini Toolbar. The selected word will be unbolded.
✳ The Mini Toolbar stays put so you can make additional changes.
✳ Change the font.
✳ Change the size.
✳ Close Word

NOTE: The font gallery will appear different on your computer from the illustration at the left – Word remembers the most recently used fonts and shows them at the top in a group called **Recently Used Fonts**.

You can change all other aspects of the text. You need not confine the changes to the Mini Toolbar. Clicking the desired commands in the Ribbon will work just as well.

Text Color and Highlight Color

Another feature of Word lets you print text in various colors and also allows you to mark text as if it were highlighted with a color marker. You do this by selecting the text, then click the appropriate command either on the Mini Toolbar or on the Ribbon.

Text Color

The **Font Color** tool for changing text color looks like this: Clicking on the ▼ brings up a gallery of colors. Click the desired color. The selected text will now be in this color (you can't see it until the selection highlight is removed). The underline color of the "A" will be in the color you clicked. When next you click on the "A" the selected text will be changed to that color.

Highlight Color

Similarly, you set a highlight color over selected text with the **Text Highlight Color** command. See the illustration here.

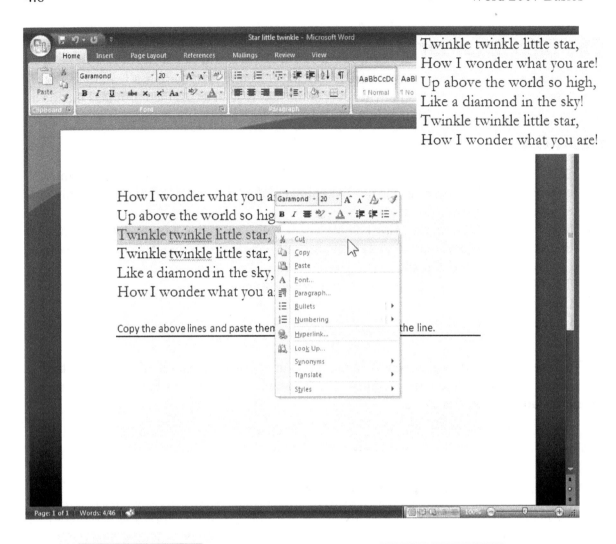

Twinkle twinkle little star,
How I wonder what you are!
Up above the world so high,
Like a diamond in the sky!
Twinkle twinkle little star,
How I wonder what you are!

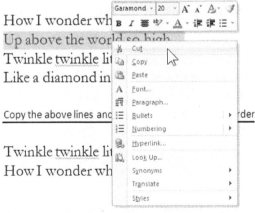

Cut, Copy and Paste

Cutting, copying and pasting are probably the most useful operations in word processing. The terms stem from the pre-computer days of publishing, when editors literally cut up texts and pasted the pieces together in the desired order. The process is much easier now; however, the names for the process have stuck. They are useful terms because it allows you to visualize the action in a manner that you have known since Kindergarten.

To cut or copy some text you need to inform Word by selecting the text. Then you need to specify where to paste it. The concept is simple enough and so is the process. In Word – and this really extends to all of computing – there are a number of ways and many variations of carrying out this action. You will learn three methods here. For your own use, you will likely prefer one of these methods.

When you *cut* selected text the text is removed from the document. It is stored on the *clipboard*. When you *copy* selected text, the text in the document is not affected. A copy of the selected text is stored on the clipboard. When you *paste,* the item that was placed last on the clipboard is inserted into the document at the cursor position.

Cut, Copy, Paste – Right-Click Method

Exercise:

* ✳ Launch Word.
* ✳ Open the file **Star little twinkle** in the **WB_PracticeFiles** folder.
* ✳ Select the first line of the poem. (Don't remember? The poem is shown superposed on the screen shot on the left.)
* ✳ With the pointer anywhere on the selected line, right-click. The Mini Toolbar and a menu will be displayed.

* ✳ In the menu click **Cut**. Notice the symbol ✂ in front of **Cut**. This is the shortcut icon for cut in almost all applications. The selected line will disappear from the document. It is now on the clipboard.
* ✳ Next right-click below the line. Again the Mini Toolbar and a menu will be shown.
* ✳ Click on **Paste** in the menu. Note that this time the cut and copy options are grayed out – they are not available because no text is selected. Also note the paste symbol 📋 – a clipboard with a sheet of paper. This symbol is also widely used as the paste shortcut. The text on the clipboard is now inserted at the place where you clicked.
* ✳ Repeat with the other lines to assemble the poem correctly.
* ✳ Close Word. No need to save the changed document.

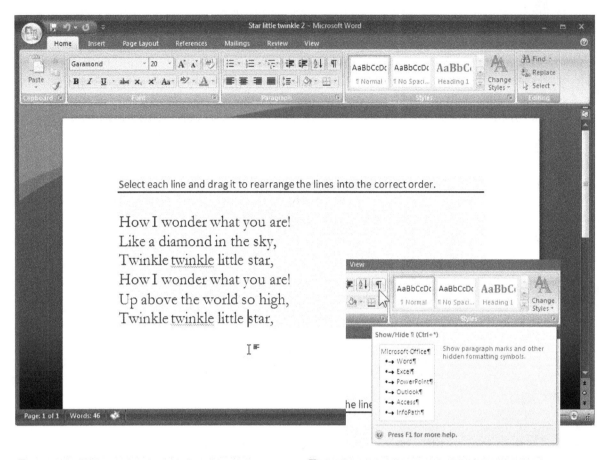

¶
How I wonder what you are! ¶
Like a diamond in the sky, ¶
Twinkle twinkle little star, ¶
How I wonder what you are! ¶
Up above the world so high, ¶
Twinkle twinkle little star, ¶

¶
How I wonder what you are! ¶
Like a diamond in the sky, ¶
Twinkle twinkle little star, ¶
How I wonder what you are! ¶
Up above the world so high, ¶
Twinkle twinkle little star, ¶
¶

Show/Hide Formatting Symbols

To keep track of the details of a document Word uses hidden formatting symbols. You can show these symbols (not really all of them) to help you in editing text. Start with an exercise to illustrate a problem and the solution.

Exercise:

* Launch Word and load the **Star little twinkle 2** file located in the **WB_PracticeFiles** folder. The file is quite similar to the one used in the last exercise.
* Click below the last line.

Can't do it, can you? The cursor is placed **in** the last line, approximately above the position where you clicked. See illustration at left. The reason is that the document ends at the last line of the text. It is not possible to place the cursor beyond the end of the document. The pointer is also "adorned" with some lines when it is past the end of the document.

Showing the hidden formatting symbols allows us to see the paragraph marks (and some other marks – for instance, there is a little dot in place of each space).

Exercise:

* Click the **Show/Hide** command, ¶ , in the **Paragraph** group on the **Home** tab.

Now the formatting symbols are shown like in the picture at the bottom left on the facing page.

Exercise:

* Click to the right of the last line. This places the cursor at the end of the document.
* Press **Enter** twice. With each press a new paragraph is started. Since there is no text on these lines the paragraph marks will be at the left margin.

Now you know how useful this feature can be. You are also ready to continue with cut, copy and paste exercises.

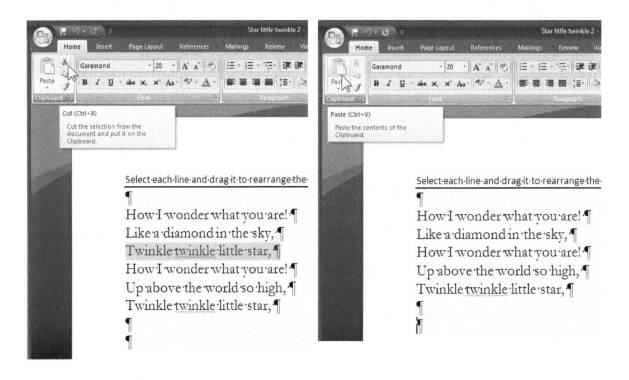

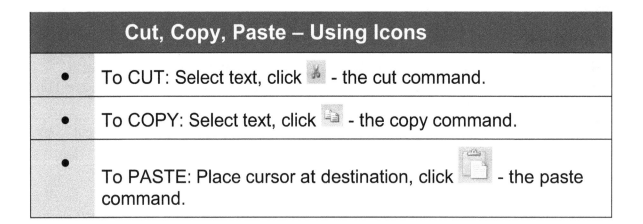

Cut, Copy, Paste – Using Icons
• To CUT: Select text, click ✄ - the cut command.
• To COPY: Select text, click ▤ - the copy command.
• To PASTE: Place cursor at destination, click ▥ - the paste command.

Cut, Copy and Paste – Using Icons

Most applications provide shortcut icons for the cut, copy and paste operations. Word locates these icons in the **Clipboard** group on the **Home** tab. When no text is selected (and with nothing on the clipboard) these commands are grayed out indicating that they are not available. The picture here shows this.

Now repeat the previous exercise, but use the commands on the Ribbon to do the cutting and pasting.

Exercise:

* Select the first actual line of the poem (use the third line as you start).
* Click the **Cut** command, ✂ , in the **Clipboard** group.
* Click the end of the document, the lowest paragraph mark.

* Click the **Paste** command, 📋 , in the **Clipboard** group. Click on the clipboard picture. If you click lower you will get a small options menu.
* Repeat with the other lines to assemble the poem correctly.
* Click the **Show/Hide** command in the Ribbon to turn the marks off.
* Admire your work!

Exercise:

* Close Word. Do not save.
* Launch Word again and reload the **Star little twinkle 2** file from the **WB_PracticeFiles** folder.
* Repeat the above exercise, but instead of using **Cut** use the **Copy** command.
* You will retain the original text and build the corrected poem below it.
* Close Word.

Cut
• Select text.
• Press **Ctrl+X**.

Copy
• Select text.
• Press **Ctrl+C**.

Paste
• Place cursor to destination location.
• Press **Ctrl+V**.

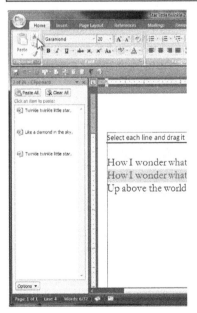  

Cut, Copy Past – Using Shortcut Keys

You probably noticed when hovering the pointer over the Cut, Copy, or Paste commands the ScreenTips boxes not only explain the function of the command, but also give the shortcut key instructions. Here they are again:

 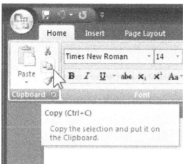 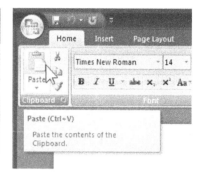

Repeat the previous exercise, this time using the shortcut keys.

Exercise:

* Launch Word and load the **Star little twinkle 2** file from the **WB_PracticeFiles** folder.
* Select the correct first line of the poem.
* Press **Ctrl+X**.
* Press **Ctrl+End**. This gets you to the end of the document.
* Press **Ctrl+V**.
* Repeat with the other lines.
* Close Word. Do not save document.

One more exercise to show how the clipboard works.

Exercise:

* Launch Word and load the **Star little twinkle 2** file from the **WB_PracticeFiles** folder.
* Click the **Dialog Box Launcher**, , in the **Clipboard** group. This shows the contents of the clipboard on the left of the Word window.
* Select one line at a time and press **Ctrl+X**. Notice how the cut lines now appear in the clipboard.
* Place the curser a couple of lines down by pressing **Enter** a couple of times.
* In the clipboard pane click on the correct first line.
* Click on the other lines in correct order. Note how the poem is now assembled in the Word window in the correct order. Admire!
* Close Word. Do not save the document.

How I wonder what you are!
Like a diamond in the sky,
Twinkle twinkle little star,
How I wonder what you are!
Up above the world so high,
Twinkle twinkle little star,

How I wonder what you are!
Like a diamond in the sky,
Twinkle twinkle little star,
How I wonder what you are!
Up above the world so high,
Twinkle twinkle little star,

How I wonder what you are!
Like a diamond in the sky,
Twinkle twinkle little star,
How I wonder what you are!
Up above the world so high,
Twinkle twinkle little star,

Twinkle twinkle little star,

How I wonder what you are!
Like a diamond in the sky,
Twinkle twinkle little star,
How I wonder what you are!
Up above the world so high,

Dragging Text

Cutting and pasting works in all condition. In some situations, however, it is easier to drag text from one position to another. The process is simple:

Dragging Text
• Select the text to be moved.
• Place the pointer anywhere on the selected text.
• Drag the text to the desired location.

While you drag the text – by holding down the left mouse button – the pointer will now look like an arrow pointer with a box attached to it – ⬚ – and a dashed vertical line – ┊ – will indicate the target location. An exercise will show this easier.

Exercise:

* Launch Word and load the **Star little twinkle 2** file from the **WB_PracticeFiles** folder.
* Select the last line: place the pointer to the left of the line and click.
* Move the pointer to anywhere on the selected line.
* Press the left mouse button down and hold it while you move the pointer to the space above the first line. The illustration at the left will help.
* Release the mouse button when the dashed vertical line is above the word "How" in the first line. The selected text will move to this position.
* Continue to finish the poem.
* Close Word. No need to save the document.

How I

You can move any selected text this way, a word, even a letter or two, whole lines as you just demonstrated, or paragraphs. If text is to be moved within the screen area, this may be the easiest way.

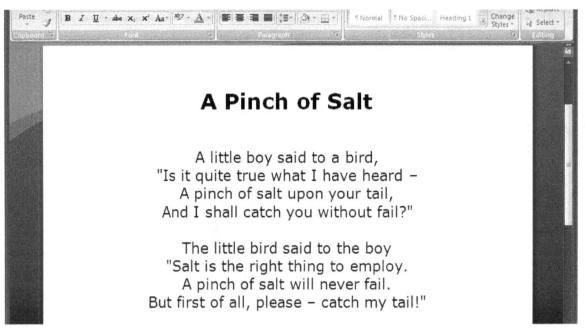

A Pinch of Salt

A little boy said to a bird,
"Is it quite true what I have heard –
A pinch of salt upon your tail,
And I shall catch you without fail?"

The little bird said to the boy
"Salt is the right thing to employ.
A pinch of salt will never fail.
But first of all, please – catch my tail!"

Centered text

A little boy said to a bird,
"Is it quite true what I have heard –
A pinch of salt upon your tail,
And I shall catch you without fail?"

The little bird said to the boy
"Salt is the right thing to employ.
A pinch of salt will never fail.
But first of all, please – catch my tail!"

Left aligned

A little boy said to a bird,
"Is it quite true what I have heard –
A pinch of salt upon your tail,
And I shall catch you without fail?"

The little bird said to the boy
"Salt is the right thing to employ.
A pinch of salt will never fail.
But first of all, please – catch my tail!"

Right aligned

A   little   boy   said   to   a   bird,
"Is   it   quite   true   what   I   have   heard   –
A   pinch   of   salt   upon   your   tail,
And   I   shall   catch   you   without   fail?"

The   little   bird   said   to   the   boy
"Salt   is   the   right   thing   to   employ.
A   pinch   of   salt   will   never   fail.
But first of all, please – catch my tail!"

Justified text – not always the best way!

Text Alignment

Text is most commonly "left-aligned", meaning that each line starts at the left margin. The right ends of the line tend to be ragged. Text in this manual is left-aligned. Sometimes it is desirable to either center the text, so that each line has the same amount of space on either side, or to "right-align" it, with all the lines ending on the right margin and looking ragged on the left side. Another option, often seen in newspapers, is "justified' text. This yields text that is set even with both the left and right margins. Space is added between words to accomplish the correct spacing.

Text alignment is controlled with the alignment commands in the **Paragraph** group on the **Home** tab.

The command icons look like this: 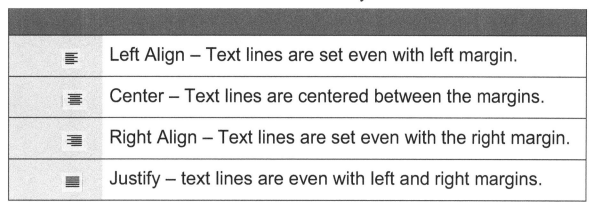 When Word starts left-align is already selected. These controls function like radio buttons – only one at a time can be selected.

≣	Left Align – Text lines are set even with left margin.
≣	Center – Text lines are centered between the margins.
≣	Right Align – Text lines are set even with the right margin.
≣	Justify – text lines are even with left and right margins.

Alignment is best illustrated with an exercise. The text of the little rhyme which you will load is all just one paragraph but with line breaks to make this demo a bit easier. As loaded the text is centered.

Exercise:

* Launch Word and load the file **A Pinch of Salt** from the **WB_PracticeFiles** folder.
* Scroll down a bit if necessary to show all of the rhyme. See picture at left.
* Click anywhere in the text.
* Click the **Align Text Left** command. Inspect the result.
* Click the **Align Text Right** command. See what happened.
* Click the **Center** command.
* Click the **Justify** command. For this example not very pretty.
* Close Word.

Lesson Four Review Questions

A. Which of the following methods are not correct ways to cut text?

1. Select the text and press **Delete**.
2. Select text and press **Ctrl+X**.
3. Select text and press **Alt-H-X**.
4. Select text, right-click and click ✂ .
5. Select text and click ✂ in the **Clipboard** group on the **Home** tab.
6. Select text and press the **Space** bar.

[For answers see pages4.9, 4.13 and 4.15]

B. What is the ¶ command used for?

1. To place special marks into legal documents.
2. To end a paragraph and start a new one.
3. To show or hide formatting symbols.
4. To switch to the Cyrillic or Greek character set.

[For answer, see page 4.11]

C. What is the ≡ command used for?

1. To increase the spacing between lines.
2. To insert grid lines into the document.
3. To make margins even.
4. To indent the paragraph.

[For answer, see page 4.19]

D. What does this ┊ symbol indicate?

1. The insertion point for typing.
2. The normal text position of the mouse pointer.
3. The insertion point for dragged text.
4. The insertion point for copied text.

[For answer, see page 4.17]

Answers: A – 1 and 6, B – 3, C – 3, D – 3.

5. More on the Home Tab

In this lesson you will learn ...

- *More on bullet and numbered lists;*
- *About Styles and Themes;*
- *How to find and replace text.*

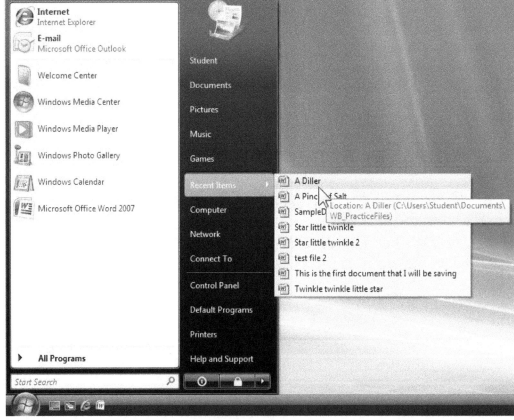

Open Document – from Recent Lists

You have learned to open a document by launching Word, then clicking the Office button, clicking Open and then navigating in the Open dialog to the desired file.In this lesson you will learn a couple of ways of opening a file that you used recently.

When you click the Office button there are a number of commands on the left. In the right pane are the names of recently used documents. In the following exercise you load three documents by using the normal open routine. This is to make sure that Word knows what the most recently used files are. After that you can try a quicker way to open a recently used file.

Exercise:

* Launch Word. Click the **Office** button. Click **Open**.
* Double-click the **WB_PracticeFiles** folder to open it.
* Double-click on **A Diller**.
* Click the **Office** button. Click **Open** and load **A Pinch of Salt**.
* Click the **Office** button. Click **Open** and load **Twinkle twinkle little star**.
* Now close all Word windows. You opened three documents so there are three Word windows open – close them all.

Open from Recent Documents in Word

Exercise:

* Launch Word.
* Click the Office button.

Note the right pane (similar to the picture on the left). The most recent documents are show. The last one you opened is at the top. You can click on the name of a document to open it.

* Close Word.

Open from Recent Items List

Here is one more way. There is a similar recent list in the Start menu. This one is organized in alphabetic order.

Exercise:

* Click **Start**
* Click **Recent Items** in the right pane. A small menu shows recent items. Just click on the one you want.

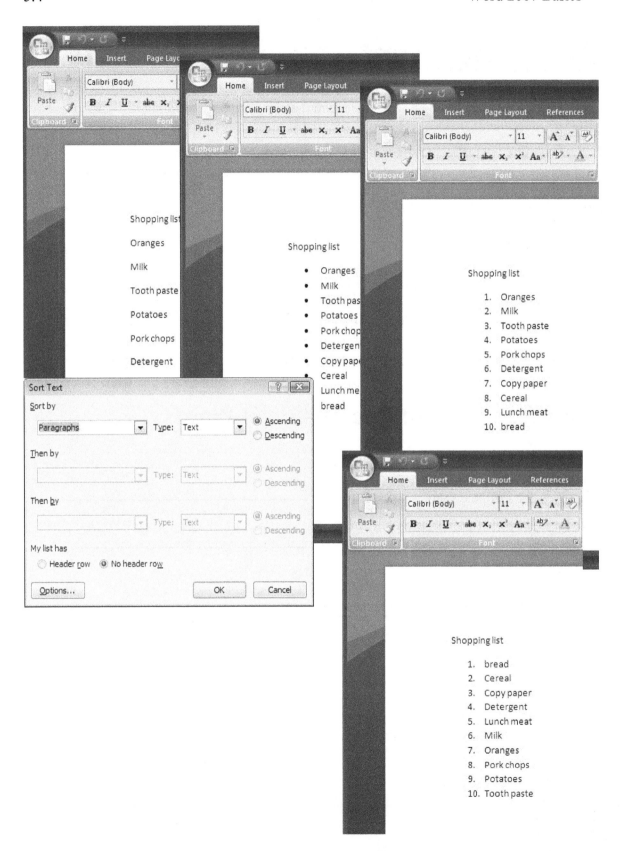

More Paragraph Formatting

Now you will learn about formatting of a list. So first you will need a list.

Exercise:
* Start Word.
* Type **shopping list**. Press the **Enter** key.
* Type about eight to ten items as they come to mind. Press the **Enter** key after each item to put it on a line of its own. If you can't think of things to buy copy the list on the left.

Bullet List

Exercise:
* Select all lines except the first one (the list title).
* Click the **Bullets** command in the **Paragraph** group on the **Home** tab.

Numbered List

Exercise:
* Select all the lines except the first one (the title).
* Click the **Numbering** command in the **Paragraph** group on the **Home** tab.

The result is a numbered list as seen on the left.

Sorting

Another very useful tool is the Sort command. This too is best illustrated with an exercise.

Exercise:
* Select all lines except the first one (the list title).
* Click the **Sort** command in the **Paragraph** group on the **Home** tab.
* Accept the settings in the Sort Text dialog by clicking **OK**.

The list is now sorted and still in numerical order.

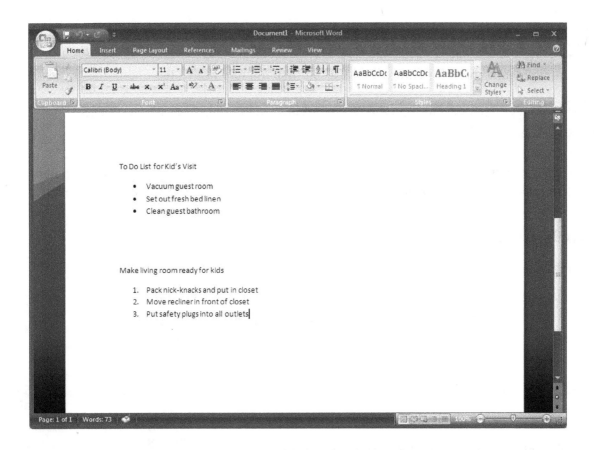

Automatic Bullet List

● Start line with an **asterisk** and **space** then type text.

Automatic Numbered List

● Start line with a **digit**, **period**, **space** then type text.

Automatic Lettered List

● Start line with a **letter**, **period**, **space** then type text.

Create a List as You Type

Word has a bit of intelligence built in. This can be very useful, but sometimes it gets in the way. Creating lists is such a frequent occurrence that Word tries to help you on the fly. Continue with the shopping list document in the following exercise.

Exercise:

* Use the **Ctrl+End** command to go to the end of the document.
* Press the **Enter** key. Word will put "11. " on the next line for you.
* Press the **Enter** again. The number will be erased and the cursor placed at the left margin to start a normal line.
* Press the **Enter** key several more times to enter vertical space.
* Type the following text: **To Do List for Kid's Visit**.
* Press **Enter**.
* Now type the following: *** vacuum guest room**   Press **Enter**. Note that Word started a bulleted list – it also capitalized the first letter on the line.
* Continue typing: **set out fresh bed linen**   Press **Enter**.
* Type: **clean guest bathroom**   Press **Enter**. Press **Enter** again to end list.
* Press **Enter** a couple more times.
* Now type: **make living room ready for kids**   Press **Enter**.
* Type: **1. pack knick-knacks and put in closet** Press **Enter**.
* Type: **move recliner in front of closet** Press **Enter**.
* Type: **put safety plugs into all outlets** Press **Enter**.

Well you get the idea. See the boxes on the left for the general procedures.

Exercise:

* Press **Ctrl+Home** to get to the top of the document for the next exercise.

Styles

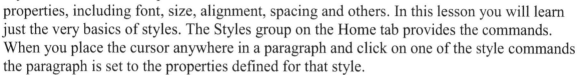

Word has another very powerful set of tools for formatting paragraphs called *styles*. Styles are named sets of predefined properties, including font, size, alignment, spacing and others. In this lesson you will learn just the very basics of styles. The Styles group on the Home tab provides the commands. When you place the cursor anywhere in a paragraph and click on one of the style commands the paragraph is set to the properties defined for that style.

Normally the Ribbon shows a few of the styles in the Styles group. As you resize the word window fewer or more styles will be displayed. To see the whole gallery of styles, click on the **More** command, 🔽 , on the right end of the style tiles that are shown. The picture on the left shows the gallery of styles. For this an exercise is essential.

Exercise:

* Select the title line.
* Click the **More** button in the **Styles** group on the **Home** tab. The styles gallery will be displayed.
* Now move the pointer around in the styles gallery and watch what happens in the text window. As you come to a style, the title line will be shown in that style.
* Click on the **Title** style. The title line will be set to that style and the gallery closes.

Now just a hint of even more power:

Exercise:

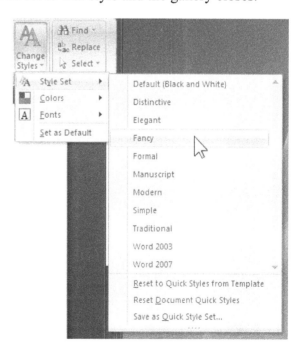

* Use the keyboard shortcut **Ctrl+A** to select the entire document.
* Click the **Change Styles** command.
* Place the pointer on **Style Set** in the little menu.
* Move the pointer into the larger menu and move it up and down over the list of style sets. Watch the text window.

The various style sets define the individual style commands differently, so a wide range of text appearance can be achieved.

You can change styles and add additional styles. Clearly another course can be built for learning this powerful toolset.

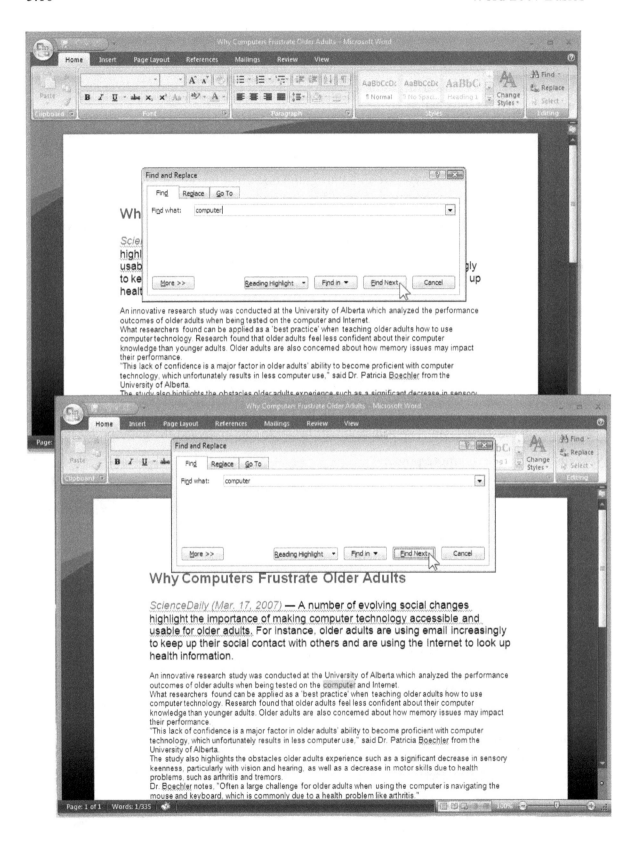

Find and Replace

Sometimes you wish to find a certain word or phrase in a document, sometimes you need to change a word or phrase to another. The *Find* and *Replace* commands help with those tasks.

Find

Exercise:

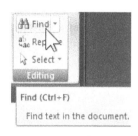

* Close Word.
* Launch Word and load **Why Computers Frustrate Older Adults** from the **WB_PracticeFiles** folder.
* Click the **Find** command in the **Editing** group on the **Home** tab. The Find and Replace dialog opens.
* In the **Find what:** text box enter **computer**.
* Click Find Next repeatedly. Watch how each instance of the word computer is found and highlighted (selected).

There is more to finding text. When you click **More >>** in the Find and Replace dialog you can specify a number of options.

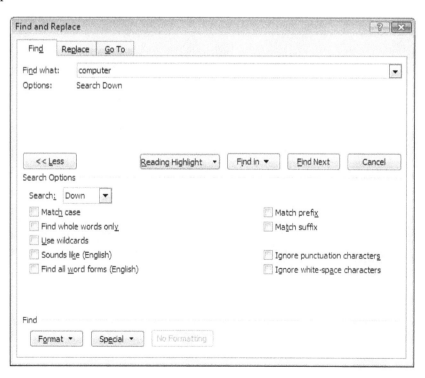

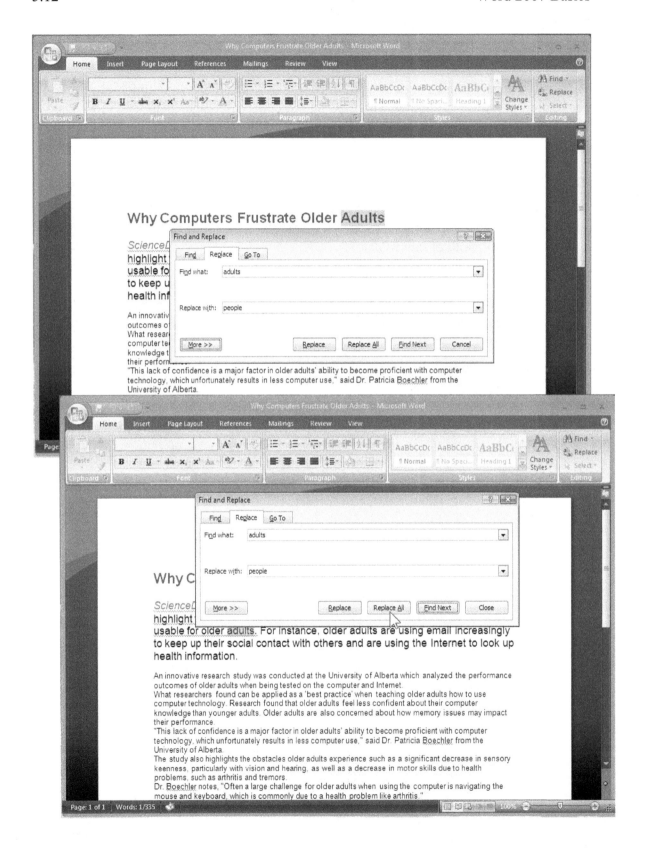

Replace

Replacing a word or phrase is just as easy. To replace text use the **Replace** command. This opens the Find and Replace dialog, but this time it has an additional text entry box, **Replace with:** for the new text that should replace the text in the **Find what:** box. Try it.

Exercise:

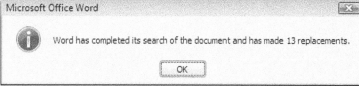

* ✱ Close any dialog boxes.
* ✱ Go to the top of the document (**Ctrl+Home**).
* ✱ Click **Replace** in the **Editing** group on the **Home** tab.
* ✱ In the **Find what:** box enter **adults**.
* ✱ In the **Replace with:** box enter **people**.
* ✱ Click **Find Next**.
* ✱ When the first instance of the word adults is found and selected click **Replace**.
* ✱ The replacement will be made and the next instance of adult will be found.
* ✱ This time click **Replace All**.

All instances of the word adults will be found and replaced with the word people. Word will report with a dialog like this:

> **Microsoft Office Word**
>
> ⓘ Word has completed its search of the document and has made 13 replacements.
>
> [OK]

* ✱ Click **OK**.
* ✱ Close Word. No need to save the document.

Lesson Five Review Questions

A. To find the bullet command you look in which ribbon group?

1. The Styles group on the Home tab.
2. The Paragraph group on the Home tab.
3. The Text group on the Insert tab.
4. The Indent group on the Page Layout tab.

[For answer, see page 5.5]

B. You can start a bullet list by typing what when starting a new line?

1. A period followed by a tab.
2. An at-symbol, @, followed by a space.
3. The letter "a" followed by a period and a space.
4. An asterisk, *, followed by a space.
5. A plus sign, +, followed by a tab.

[For answer, see page 5.7]

C. To find a word or phrase you click what command icon?

1.
2.
3.
4.
5.

[For answers, see page 5.11]

Answers: A – 2, B – 4, C – 3.

6. The Insert and Review Tabs

Lesson Six is all about inserting things ...

- *Symbols*
- *Date and time*
- *Pictures*
- *Drawings*
- *Word Art*
- *Text boxes*
- *Tables*

Insert Text Symbol
• Click **Insert** tab.
• In **Symbols** group click **Insert Symbol**.
• Click on symbol if it is in menu,
• otherwise click **More Symbols** and click on symbol in table.

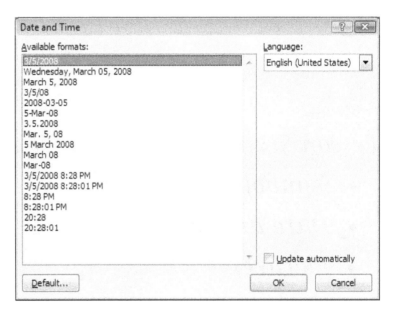

Adrop cap at the beginning of a paragraph can be used to avoid a full page of text in a document from appearing "gray" and monotonous. Of course the whole document should follow a consistent style. This is often employed in books and magazines, rarely in short, informal documents.

The Insert Tab

The Insert tab provides commands and tools for inserting a variety of items into your document. There are many more tools than can be covered in this course. Here you will get acquainted with just a few of them.

Inserting Symbols into Text

On many occasions the letters, digits and symbols shown on the keyboard are not enough to present the idea or information you wish to convey. You might need such symbols as Greek letters, arrows, mathematical signs and others. The fonts installed on your computer provide a great many such symbols.

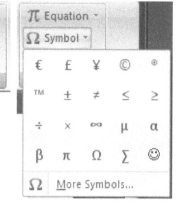

Such symbols are reached on the **Insert** tab in the **Symbols** group. To insert a symbol click on the **Insert Symbol** command. If you have recently inserted a symbol, it will be shown on a small gallery. To select another symbol click on **More Symbols …** . When you click the **Equation** command, an entire new tab is presented. Inserting mathematical equations is beyond the scope of this course.

Inserting Date and Time

The **Text** group on the **Insert** tab provides a command to insert the current date or time. To insert date or time click the Insert date and Time command. In the dialog box select the format you prefer. See the picture on the left.

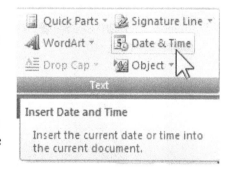

Note: There is a check box on the Date and Time dialog labeled **Update automatically**. When this is checked, the date or time in the document is updated to the current date or time when the document is opened.

Drop Cap

Another neat feature is the **Drop Cap** command. This sets the first letter or word in a larger size at the beginning of a paragraph. This command is also located in the **Text** group on the **Insert** tab. Select the letter or word to be placed in a larger font, then click the **Drop Cap** command and click on **Dropped** or another option. **Drop Cap Options** allows you to specify font and size (in number of lines) and spacing to the text.

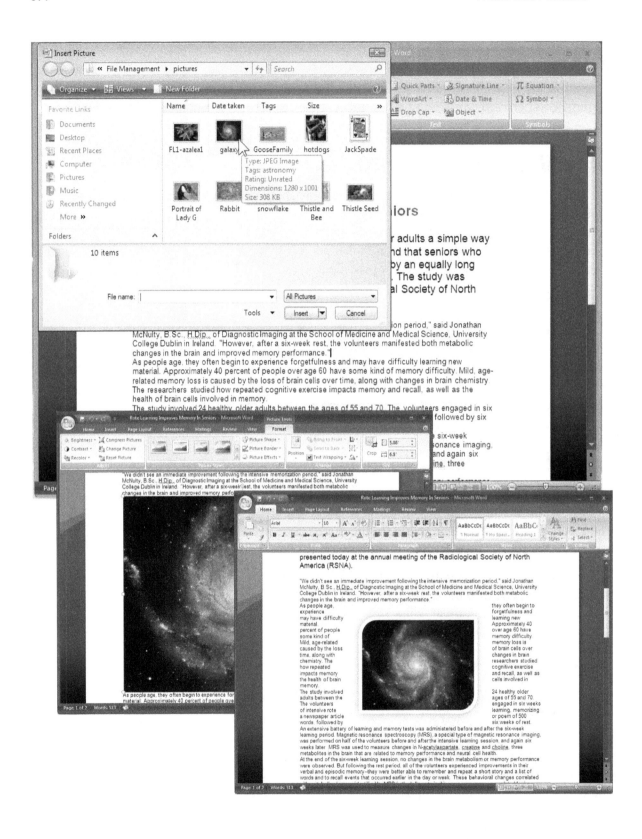

Inserting Pictures

Illustrations and photographs can be essential for a document to present the intended information. Inserting pictures is something you will likely want to do quite often. In Word this is also quite simple.

Exercise:

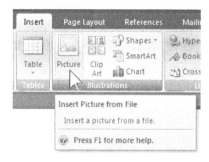

* Start Word and load **Rote Learning Improves Memory in Seniors** from the **WB_PracticeFiles** folder.
* Click at the end of the first small text paragraph .
* Click the **Insert** tab.
* In the **Illustrations** group click **Insert Picture from File**. The Insert Picture dialog opens showing the Pictures folder contents.
* In the navigation pane click **Documents**. In the contents pane double-click **WB_PracticeFiles**, then double-click **File Management**, and finally double-click **pictures**. Find and click on **galaxy**.
* Click **Insert**.

The picture is inserted and a new tab is added to the Ribbon. The new tab displays tools for managing the picture. There are many options than will not be covered in this course. Important controls are size and positioning in text. You will also learn a little about *Picture Styles*.

Exercise:

* In the **Size** group click on the **Shape Width** down arrow until the box show **3"**. Watch the picture change size as you click repeatedly to get down to the desired size.

* In the **Arrange** group click **Text Wrapping**.
* In the drop down menu click **Square**. Notice how the text is now wrapped around the picture on the right.
* Click on the picture. Notice the four-arrow pointer.
* Drag the picture a ways down and to the right. Notice how text is wrapped all around the picture.
* In the **Picture Styles** group move the pointer slowly over the little pictures. Notice how the appearance of the picture changes as you move from one style to another. Click to display a gallery of more styles. Move the pointer slowly over the little pictures and observe how the picture in the text changes. When you find the style you like, click on it.

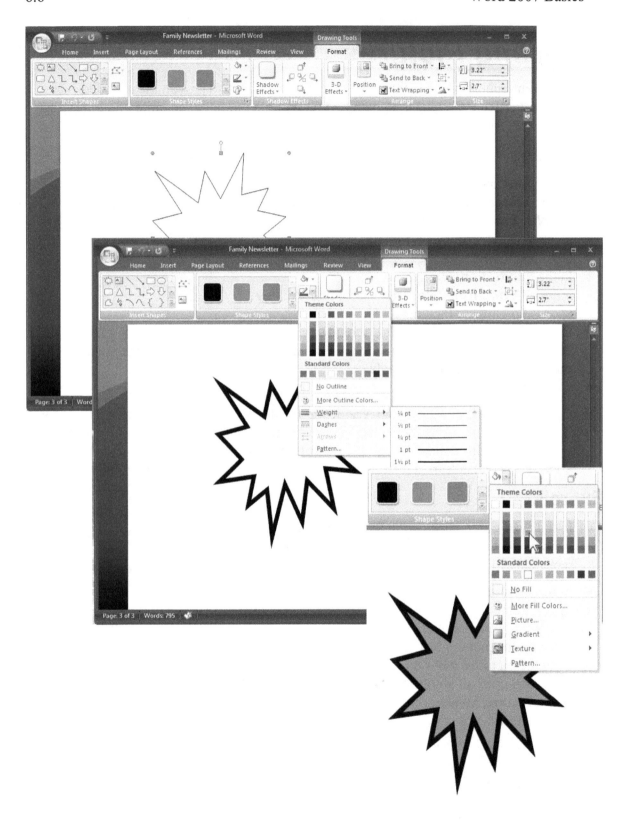

Inserting Drawings and Shapes

Word provides a number of shapes that you can place into a document. All the shapes can be changed in size, color and other characteristics.

Exercise:

* Scroll down in the open document to fill the screen with blank lines. Use the **Enter** key if needed to make more blank lines.
* On the **Insert** tab, in the **Illustrations** group click **Shapes**. A gallery of shapes opens.
* In the **Stars and Banners** section click on the first one, **Explosion 1**.
* Place the pointer, which is now a + shape, towards the left top. Drag (press and hold the left mouse button and move the mouse) towards the lower right. Notice how the shape is drawn and increased in size. The **Drawing Tools** tab appears with formatting options.
* In the **Shape Styles** group click **Shape Outline**.
* In the gallery click on **Weight**.
* In the new menu click **6 pt**. The width of the lines gets wider.
* Click **Shape Fill**.
* Move the pointer slowly over the colors in the gallery and watch the shape being filled with the different colors. When you get to one you like, click on it.
* When you are finished close Word, do not save the file.

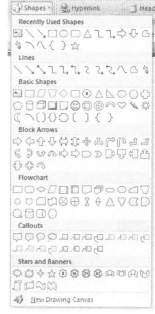

Note: The **Drawing Tools** tab appears when you click on the drawing. It is not available when you are elsewhere in the document.

The **Scribble** tool, , is used like a pencil. Use it for free-hand drawings like this:

There are many more options and features you will want to explore. Enjoy!

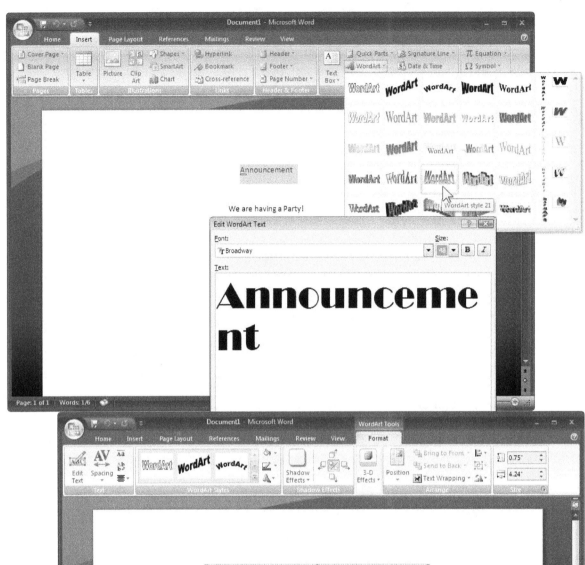

WordArt

Word allows you to modify the design and appearance of text with a set of tools called WordArt. You can use decorative text in signs, announcements, cards, and similar uses. You reach **WordArt** on the **Insert** tab in the **Text** group.

Exercise:

* Launch Word.
* Click **Center** in the **Paragraph** group on the **Home** tab.
* Type: **Announcement**. Press **Enter** twice.
* Type: **We are having a Party!** End the paragraph with **Enter**.
* Select the first line.
* Click **WordArt** in the **Text** group on the **Insert** tab.
* Click on a style you like. The Edit WordArt Text dialog comes up.
* In the **Font:** box scroll down and click on **Broadway**.
* In the **Size:** box select **48**.
* Click **OK**. The text will be changed according to your selection.

The WordArt Tools tab, **WordArt Tools Format**, appears whenever a WordArt item is selected. Here you can modify the text in many ways.

Exercise:

* Have fun playing with the text. Select the second line and convert it to WordArt. Enjoy!
* Close Word when you are finished, no need to save.

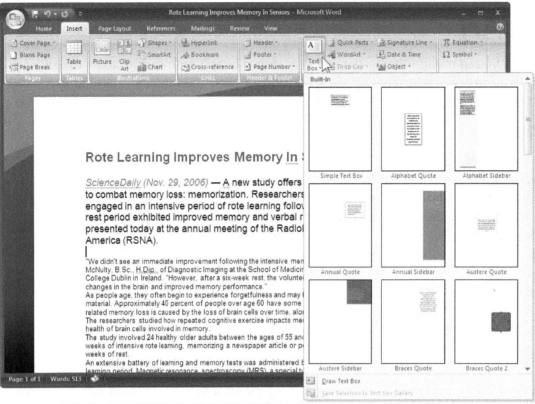

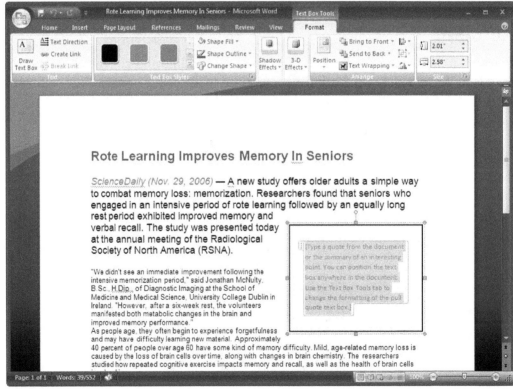

Text Box

A text box is just that, a box with text in it. Text boxes are often used for supplementary information. They are very popular in magazines.

Exercise:

✱ Launch Word and load the file **Rote Learning Improves Memory In Seniors** from the **WB_PracticeFiles** folder.

✱ Click the **Insert** tab, then **Text Box** in the **Text** group. The Built-In text box gallery opens.

✱ Select one of the designs and click on it.

A text box is inserted and the Text Box Tools tab appears. This tab is available whenever a text box is selected. It provides an array of tools for modifying the text box.

Tables

Tables are another very useful tool for presenting information. Take a quick look.

Exercise:

✱ Place the cursor at the beginning of a paragraph.

✱ Click **Table** in the **Tables** group on the **Insert** tab.

✱ Drag the pointer across the gallery to specify the number of columns and rows. As you do so the table will appear in the text and change according to the pointer position.

✱ Release the pointer to complete the process.

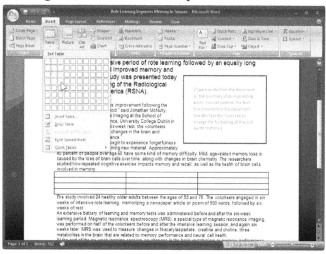

Two tabs are now available to manipulate the table, **Table Tools Design** and **Table Tools Layout**.

Here is an example of a word that is offen misspelled.

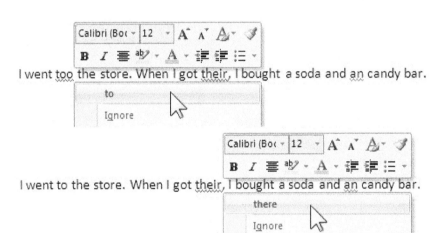

I went too the store. When I got their, I bought a soda and an candy bar.

The Review Tab

The Review tab offers the Spelling & Grammar command. This is probably one of the most important features. Even without going to the Review tab Word automatically performs spelling, grammar and usage checking for you.

Automatic Error Correction

By default Word automatically corrects a large number of words when you mistype them. For example when you type *adn* it instantly corrects it to *and*. It has a large catalog of frequently mistyped words and corrects them as you type.

As you type Word checks each word for spelling and performs grammar and usage checking. It indicates suspicious words or phrases with wavy underlines.

Red Wavy Underlines

Word flags words it does not recognize or thinks might be misspelled with a wavy red line. When you see a wavy red line, right-click on the word. In the little menu you will likely see the word you meant to use, just click it and the incorrect word will be replaced.

In the example on the left the word *often* is misspelled. Right-clicking on the underlined word offers a list of possible correct words.

Green Wavy Underline

Word uses a green wavy underline to mark text it thinks is grammatically incorrect. For some phrases it offers a revision, for others just an explanation of what it thinks might be wrong.

Blue Wavy Underline

Blue wavy underlines are used on words that Word thinks are incorrectly used.

Exercise:

* ✳ Open Word.
* ✳ Type the following, just as shown here: **I went too the store. When I got their, I bought a soda adn an candy bar.**
* ✳ Note that the word *and* was corrected immediately. Three others are marked.
* ✳ Right-click on each underlined word in turn. Note the offered word in the menu. Click on the proper word to correct the text.
* ✳ Close Word when you are done. Do not save the document.

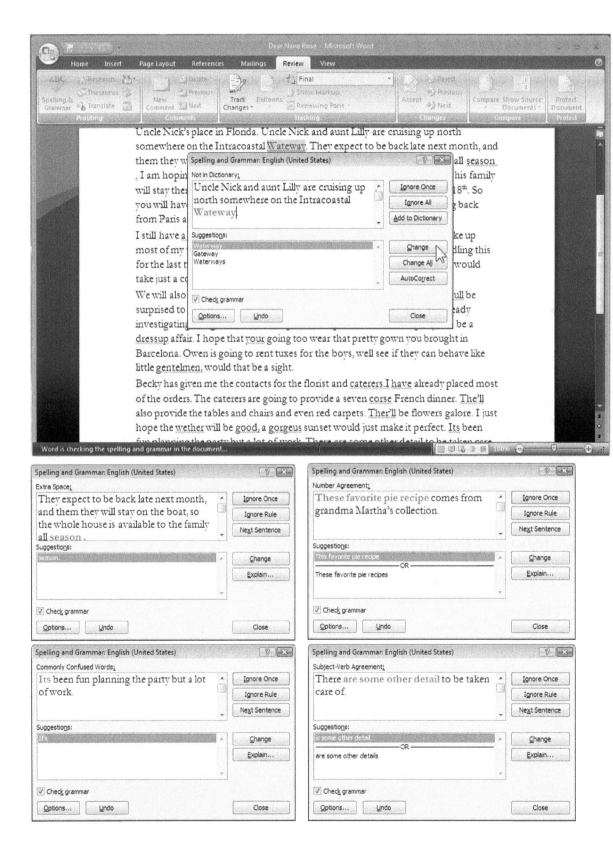

Spelling and Grammar Checking

You can make corrections as you go along entering text. You can also perform the checking on an entire document. You can learn about this from the following example.

Exercise:

* Launch Word and load **Dear Nana Rose** from the **WB_PracticeFiles** folder.
* Click the **Review** tab.
* Click **Spelling & Grammar** in the **Proofing** group.

The Spelling and Grammar dialog comes up. It shows the portion of the text with the suspect error. The top line indicates the possible error. The first dialog reports: "**Capitalization:**" The next one (top illustration) says "**Not in Dictionary:**" – this is a possible spelling error – indeed that is the case in the example. The text contains "Wateway" which should read "Waterway". An easily overlooked error.

In the **Suggestions:** box it offers a possible correct word or words. If the offered word is correct, as it is in the illustration:

* Click **Change**. The checking continues to the next possible error.
* Continue with the checking, making corrections as appropriate.

Note that some of the possible errors are not errors at all. You still need to examine the situation and decide on the correct action. **Ignore Once** may be the appropriate course.

The document contains a wide variety of different errors and text that Word finds suspect. Notice the place where "**Extra Space:**" was found, also "**Comma Usage:**".

* Examine each dialog carefully. Making corrections when needed.
* When you are finished, close Word. Do not save the document!

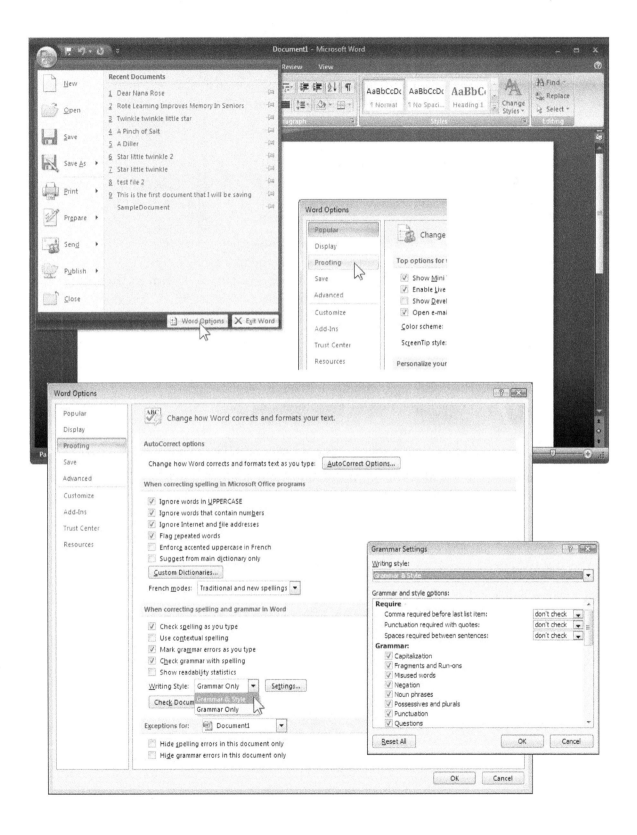

Style Checking

Word can do some style checking. That is not turned on by default. In the next exercise you will turn on style checking and then examine the Dear Nana Rose document again.

Exercise:

* ✳ Launch Word.
* ✳ Click the **Office Button**.
* ✳ Click **Word Options** (bottom of dialog).
* ✳ Click **Proofing**.
* ✳ In the group **When correcting spelling and grammar in Word** find **Writing Style:** Click the ▼ next to **Grammar Only** and click on **Grammar & Style** in the little menu.
* ✳ Next click on **Settings...** - See the many options in the Grammar Settings dialog.
* ✳ You can set many options. For now just click **OK**.
* ✳ Click **OK** to close the Word Options dialog.
* ✳ Click the **Office Button** again.
* ✳ Note the listing of the most recent documents. You can open a document by clicking the name or by pressing the number key corresponding to the number in front of the document name. Press **1**.

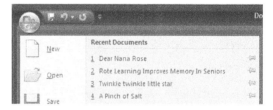

Now do the Spelling and Grammar check again. This time you will see many more error reports.

Exercise:

* ✳ Click the **Review** tab.
* ✳ Click **Spelling & Grammar**.

Notice that the first error is "Wordiness:".

* ✳ Continue through the document.
* ✳ When you are finished, close Word. Do not save the file (so you can do this exercise again).

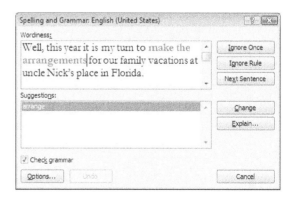

Odds and Ends

Here are a few items that may come in handy now and then.

Inserting Dashes

There are three different dashes that are used in printed text.

The Hyphen

The hyphen is used in some word combinations like e-mail and at the end of a line when a word must be split (which Word can do for you automatically). The hyphen is typed with the hyphen key on the keyboard.

The En Dash –

The en dash is a slightly longer dash – like this. Word puts it in automatically when you type a hyphen (or two) preceded and followed by a space. If you need to force the character use **Ctrl+Numpad-Minus**. If you do not have a number pad, you can insert the character from **Insert** – **Symbols** – **Symbol** – **More Symbols…** – **Special Character** then select it in the dialog.

The Em Dash —

Often a phrase is offset within a sentence in text—this is such an example—with a long dash called an em dash. Word generates an em dash when you type two hyphens without spaces between text. You can force an em dash with **Alt+Ctrl+Numpad-Minus** or from **Special Characters** as described for the en dash.

Inserting a Page Break

Sometimes you may wish to start a new page unconditionally even though there is space left on the present page. You do this with **Ctrl+Enter**.

Suppressing a Break

At times you want to continue on the next line but without starting a new paragraph. This is often needed in bullet or numbered lists. To continue on the next line use **Shift+Enter**. This will show as a ↵ symbol when **Show/Hide** is in show formatting marks mode.

Non-Break Space

Sometimes words need to be next to each other and you do not want a line break between them. In this manual many of the two-word commands, such as _**Page Layout**_, are always kept together. This is done with a non-break space, **Ctrl+Shift+Space**. This will show similar to a degree symbol when **Show/Hide** is in show formatting marks mode.

Non-Break Hyphen

When a hyphen is needed but you do not want the line to break on that hyphen use Ctrl+Shift+Hyphen. The line will not break on this symbols, but it is a little different from an actual hyphen. You can see this especially when the text size is large: will-break vs. non-break

Shortcut Keys

Throughout this course you have become acquainted with many keyboard shortcuts, normally called shortcut keys. There are many others. In addition there is a new set called Key Tips.

Key Tips

For every command in Word there is a Key Tip. To use these Key Tips you start by pressing Tab. The Ribbon will light up with little boxes showing letters or numbers, in some places multiple letters. When these are displayed press the one over the command you want. In some cases it will lead to more Key Tips being displayed. It is easier to use than to describe.

Exercise:

* Launch Word.
* Press the **Alt** key. See the Key Tips on the Ribbon.
* Press **H**. This gets you to the **Home** tab.
* Press **R**. The Find and Replace dialog pops up.
* Close Word when you are finished experimenting.

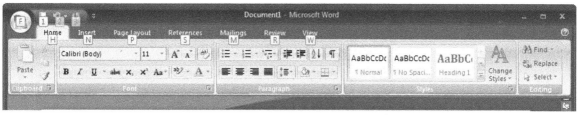

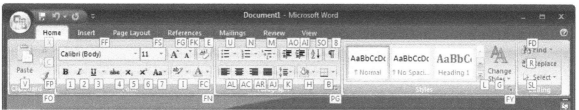

Lesson Six Review Questions

A. To find the insert date command you look in which ribbon group?

1. The Styles group on the Home tab.
2. The Paragraph group on the Home tab.
3. The Text group on the Insert tab.
4. The Indent group on the Page Layout tab.

[For answer, see page 6.3]

B. To draw a free-hand figure what command do you use?

1. WordArt in Text group on the Insert tab.
2. SmartArt in Illustrations group on the Insert tab.
3. Scribble tool under Lines in Shapes in the Illustrations group on the Insert tab.
4. Line tool under Lines in Shapes in the Illustrations group on the Insert tab.
5. Curve tool under Lines in Shapes in the Illustrations group on the Insert tab.

[For answer, see page 6.7]

C. What does a blue, wavy underline under a word mean?

1. The word is mispelled.
2. The word is not in the dictionary.
3. The word might be used incorrectly.
4. The word is an illegal swear word.

[For answer, see page 6.13]

Answers: A – 3, B – 3, C – 3.

7. Three Tabs: Page Layout, View and References

In this lesson you will get acquainted with ...

- *The Page Layout tab and some of its tools.*
- *The View tab and how a document can be displayed.*
- *The References tab that offers some very powerful tools for making your documents into professional works.*

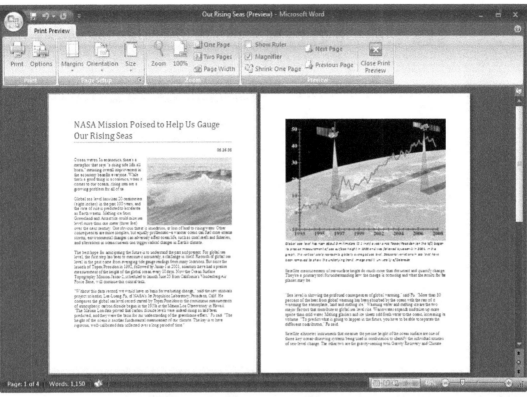

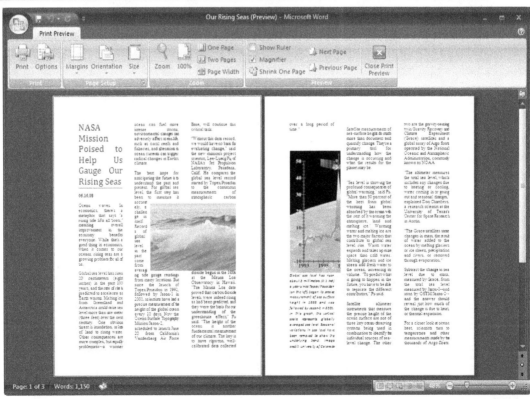

Page Layout

Laying out the text on the page so it looks good is a bit of an art. You will not learn that art in this course, but you will learn some of the tools for modifying the layout.

Exercise:

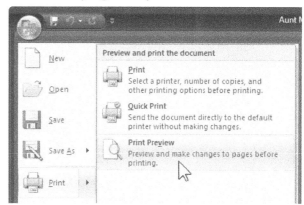

* Launch Word and load **Our Rising Seas** from the **WB_PracticeFiles** folder.
* Click the **Office** button, move the pointer over **Print**, then click on **Print Preview**. The Print Preview tab is displayed and the main pane shows how the letter would appear when printed.
* Click Two Pages in the **Zoom** group. You now see how both pages would look; similar to the picture on the left.
* Click **Close Print Preview** in the **Preview** group. This gets you back to the normal view.

Margins

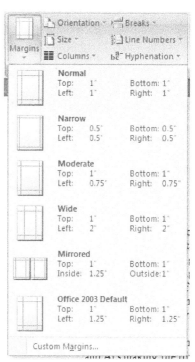

* Now click the **Page Layout** tab.
* Click **Margins** in the **Page Setup** group.
* Click **Wide** in the gallery. Inspect how the text layout has changed.
* Repeat and click **Narrow**. Observe the effect.
* Repeat and click **Normal** to return to the original.

Columns

Now for something different.

* Click **Columns** in the **Page Setup** group.
* Click **Three** in the gallery. Looks like a newspaper now.
* Now just for fun click the **Home** tab.
* In the **Editing** group (far right) click **Select**, the **Select All**.
* Click **Justify** in the **Paragraph** group.

Presto, you are in the newspaper business. Congratulations!

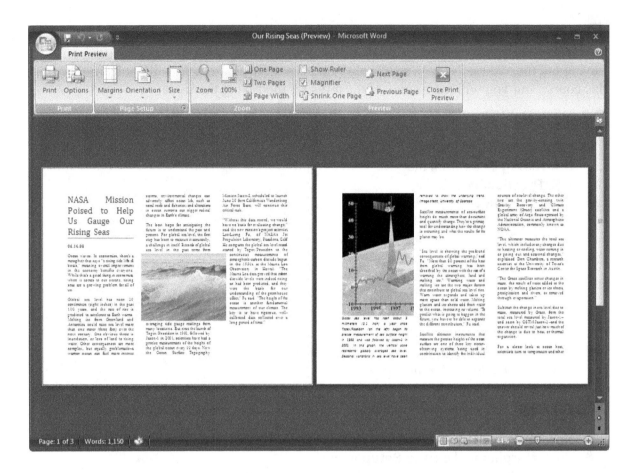

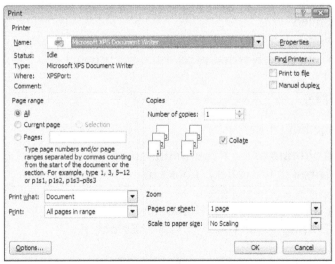

Orientation

Most text documents are printed on 8 ½ by 11 inch paper with the narrow dimension horizontal. That is called portrait orientation. When the layout is wider than high it is called landscape orientation.

Exercise:

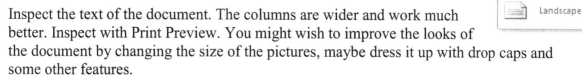

* ✻ Click **Orientation** in the **Page Setup** group. You get a choice of just two in the gallery: **Portrait** and **Landscape**.
* ✻ Click **Landscape**.

Inspect the text of the document. The columns are wider and work much better. Inspect with Print Preview. You might wish to improve the looks of the document by changing the size of the pictures, maybe dress it up with drop caps and some other features.

Printing

From page layout it is only a small step to printing. In this course, printing can only be addressed in the most rudimentary fashion. Printers and their features vary immensely. To print click the **Office** button, move the pointer to **Print** and click on **Print** in the right pane.

This brings up the Print dialog. In this dialog you select the printer – on the left the Microsoft XPS Document Writer is shown. This is a built in "printer" and is part of Windows Vista.

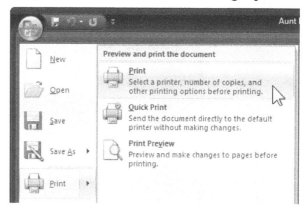

You can make the various selections – what part of the document to print, number of copies, collation, and some other properties.

The Properties button brings up a dialog that is specific to the selected printer.

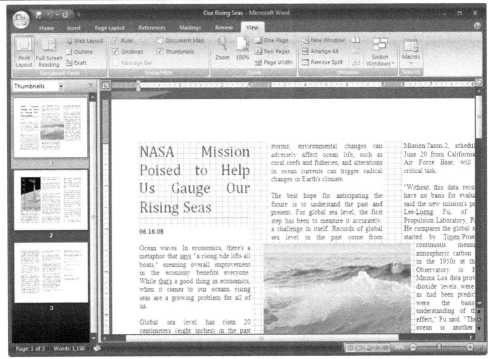

Viewing Your Document

The View tab offers some options for viewing your document. *Print Layout* view is the default. It presents the document as it will look when printed. Since there is allowance for margins, you cannot see as much text as you might like. When you just want to read the text of a document, you can set Full Screen Reading in the Document Views group on the View tab.

Exercise:

❋ Click the **View** tab.
❋ In the **Document Views** group click **Full Screen Reading**.

Word goes full screen on your monitor. The Ribbon and other controls, even the borders are removed to provide maximum space for the document. Just one thin bar remains at the top with some controls. The most important control is the **Close** button, X Close , to close the full screen mode and return to the normal view.

Show/Hide Group

The Show/Hide group on the View tab contains several commands to turn options on and off.

- **Ruler** – Turns the horizontal and vertical rulers on and off.
- **Gridlines** – Turns gridlines on and off. These can be useful when positioning pictures and other inserted items.
- **Thumbnails** – When checked this feature shows small images of the various pages in a window on the left (default).

You may wish to experiment with these. The picture on the left has these three features turned on.

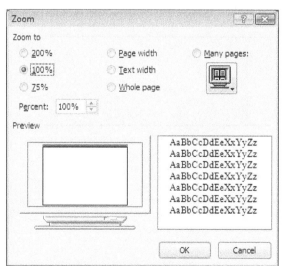

Zoom

You are already acquainted with the Zoom control at the lower right of the Word window. The **Zoom** group of the **View** tab offers some additional controls.

- **Zoom** – This control brings up a dialog with the options shown in the picture here.

Try the other commands.

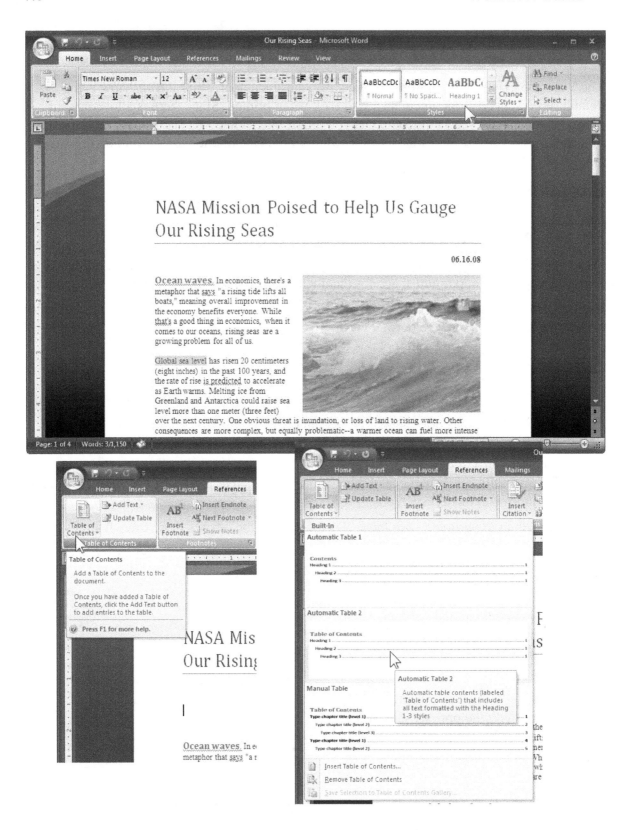

The Reference Tab

The Reference tab provides tools for building a table of contents, inserting footnotes, and citations, for creating captions for pictures and tables, and also for building an index.

Another powerful options is cross-referencing, such as "*see page 17*" with the actual page number automatically corrected. This manual uses most of these features.

Here you will get just a hint of the usefulness of some of these tools.

In the next exercise you will create a table of contents and an index. This is not the way you would want to do it for an actual publication.

Exercise:

* Launch Word and load **Our Rising Seas** from the **WB_PracticeFiles** folder.
* Select the first two words of the first paragraph, "Ocean waves", and click on **Heading 1** in the **Styles** group on the **Home** tab.
* Select the first few words of the next paragraph and click on **Heading 1**. See the illustration at the left.
* Do this for the next two paragraphs, setting the first few words in style Heading 1.

You have identified the first few words of five paragraphs as headings, Heading 1. This gives you something to work with for building a table of contents.

* Return to the start of the document with **Ctrl-Home**.
* Place the cursor in front of the first paragraph and press **Enter** several times to make space.
* Place the cursor on the second newly-made blank line.
* Click the **Reference** tab.
* Click on **Table of Contents** (in the **Table of Contents** group).
* In the gallery click on **Automatic Table 2**.

Word now builds the table of contents and inserts it into the document at the cursor position.

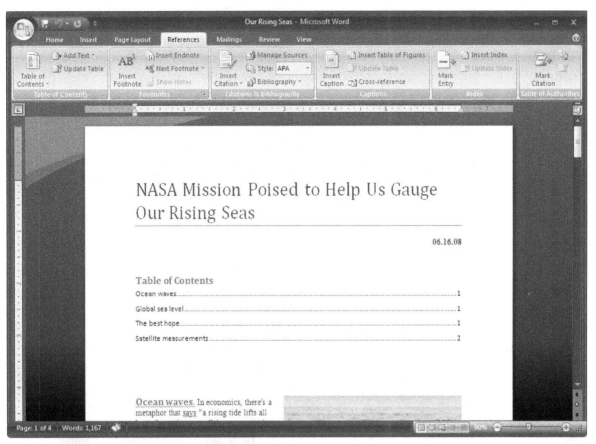

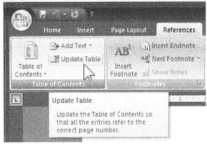

Table of Contents

In the exercise on the previous page you inserted a table of contents into the document. Now you will learn a bit more of the capability of this feature.

Exercise:

* Scroll down in the document to the first paragraph where you have not set the first words into Heading 1 style.
* Click on the **Home** tab.
* Select the first few words of the paragraph and click **Heading 1** in the **Styles** group.
* Do this for the next four paragraphs.
* Return to the start of the document (**Ctrl-Home**).
* Click the **Reference** tab.
* In the **Table of Contents** group click **Update Table**.
* In the dialog click **Update entire table**.
* Click **OK**.
* Return to the start of the Document.

Note that the newly added headings (the marked paragraphs) have been added to the table of contents.

Table of Contents

Ocean waves 1

Global sea level 1

The best hope 2

Satellite measurements 3

Satellite altimeter 3

Subtract the change 4

For a closer look 4

For example 4

This is a mystery 4

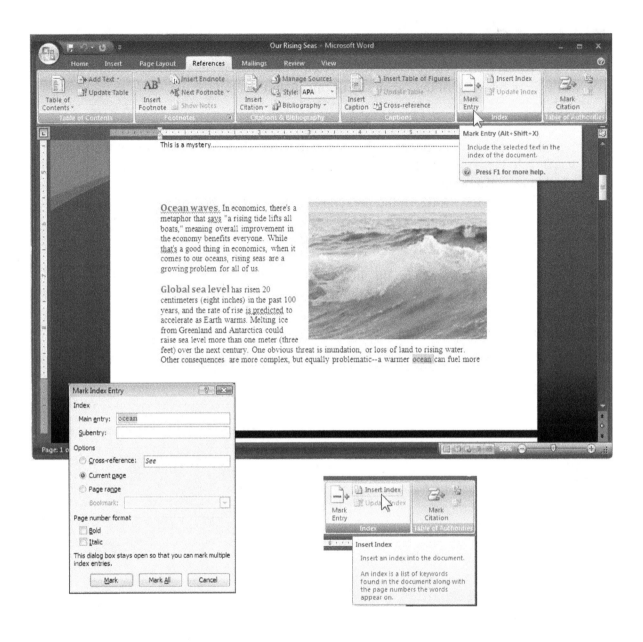

Index

In the next exercise you continue in the Our Oceans document, this time to build an index. The index built in this exercise is not a very good one, but it should get the idea across to you.

Exercise:

* Return to the start of the document if you are not already there.
* Scroll down so you can see the second paragraph (see picture at left).
* Select the word "ocean".
* Click on the **Reference** tab.
* In the **Index** group click on **Mark Entry**. The Mark Index Entry dialog opens.
* Click **Mark All**.
* Close the dialog (either with [x] or **Close**).
* In the same paragraph find the word "sea" and repeat the procedure: Click **Mark Entry**, then click **Mark All** and close the dialog.
* Click the **Home** tab.
* Click the **Show/Hide** command in the **Paragraph** group.

Word will have added hidden annotations in the text. With the Show/Hide you turned on the display of the annotations so you can see them. The entry marks will look like this:

ocean{ XE:"ocean". } , sea{ XE:"sea". } .

When you clicked Mark All, Word marked the words with the precise spelling thoughout the document. If the word occurs more than once in a paragraph, only the first occurrence is marked. If the spelling of the word is different, such as being capitalized, it is not marked. If the word is part of a word, such as :seas" or "research", those words are not marked.

You have marked a couple of words so now build the index.

Exercise:

* Go to the end of the document: press **Ctrl-End**.
* Press **Enter** a few times to make room.
* On the **Reference** tab, click **Insert Index**. The Index dialog comes up.
* Just click **OK** – don't change any of the options.

Word inserts a section break and the newly created index:

ocean, 1, 2, 3, 4, 5¶
sea, 1, 2, 3, 4, 5¶ ····· Section Break (Continuous) ·····
¶

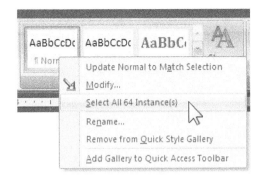

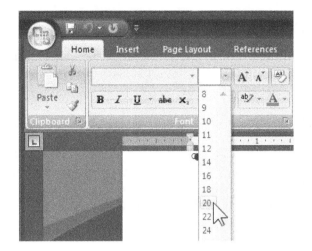

ocean, 1, 2, 3, 4, 5¶   sea, 1, 2, 3, 4, 5¶

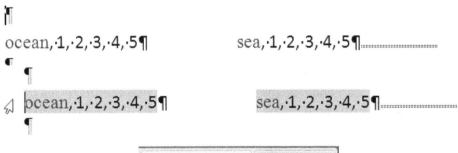

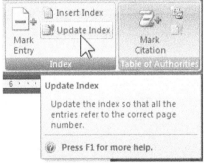

ocean, 2, 3, 4, 5, 6, 7¶   sea, 2, 3, 4, 5, 6, 7, 8¶

Reference Power Demo

For an exercise to demonstrate the power of Word, change the text size so the document now requires more pages. Update the table of contents and the index to see how Word makes references an easy chore.

Exercise:

* Click the **Home** tab.
* In the **Styles** group right-click on the **Normal** command.
* In the drop-down menu click **Select All 64 Instance(s)**.

This selects all the text in the document that is set in Normal style – pretty much most of the document.

* In the **Font** group click on the size ▾command . The size box will not show a size because in the selected text there are various size changes.
* Click on **20**. The size of all Normal text will be changed to 20 point.
* Return to the start of the document (**Ctrl-Home**).
* Click anywhere in the table of contents and move the pointer to the top of the table. An **Update Table** tab will appear as illustrated at the left.
* Click on **Update Table**.
* In the Update Table dialog click on **Update entire table**.
* Click on **OK**. The table of contents will be updated with the new page numbers.
* Go to the end of the document: press **Ctrl-End**. Note the index and the page numbers.
* Click the **Reference** tab.
* Move the pointer into the left margin in front of the index and click to select it.
* In the Index group the **Update Index** command will now be available. Click it.
* The index is now updated. You may need to scroll down to see it. It will be set in the original, smaller type. The page numbers now have been updated.
* Close Word. Do not save the document.

Lesson Seven Review Questions

A. Orientation is a term used to describe what?

1. The first speech freshmen get in college.
2. How the document is placed with respect to the paper dimensions.
3. The direction to North when you use your computer.
4. How paper is stuffed into the printer.

[For answer, see page 7.5]

B. Where is the Margin command located?

1. On the Home tab in the Paragraph group.
2. On the View tab in the Document Views group.
3. On the Page Layout tab in the Page Setup group.

[For answers, see page 7.3]

C. How do you make a table of contents?

1. You scroll through the document and write down the page numbers for each section, then you type up the information and format it as a list.
2. You locate the cursor where you want the table and click Table of Contents on the Reference tab.
3. You click the Table command on the Insert tab.

[For answer , see page 7.11]

Answers: A – 2, B – 3, C – 2.

8. The Mailings Tab

This last lesson introduces you to the Mailings tab. Some of what you can do here is to print envelopes, create labels, cards, and documents that are customized with information brought in from an external source.

This lesson also includes some review exercises.

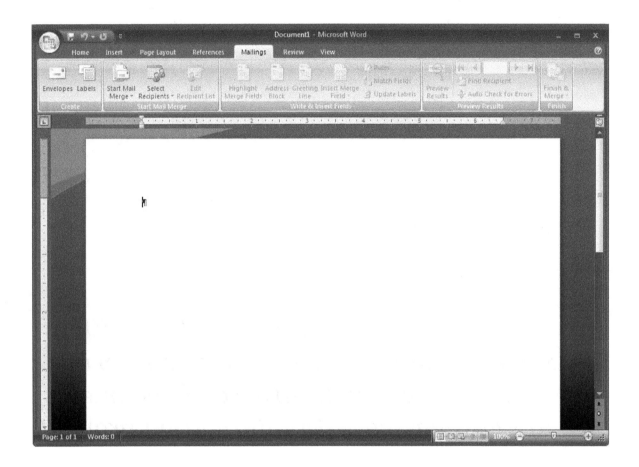

The Mailings Tab

The Mailings tab provides tools for creating labels and envelopes, and for merging text, such as names and addresses, into documents. When you click on the Mailings tab you will see all but four of the commands grayed out – not available. The first group provides for creating new envelopes or labels. The second group – Start Mail Merge – is where you will normally start a mail merge operation. This allows you to bring in information from an external file – a document or data file – and merge information from that source into a document, or set of documents. Tools in this tab become available as you progress through the mail merge process. These tools are very powerful, and are mostly beyond the scope of this book; however, you may enjoy the exercises in this lesson to give you a taste of the capabilities.

Creating Labels – setting up the details of how these items are laid out – is not covered in this book. You will most likely use commercial stock for labels, business cards and the like. These are well supported in Word and you need not "create" them.

Printing envelopes for letters you write is covered in the first exercise. Following that are exercises for merging data into documents. These also are not covered in great detail, just enough to introduce you to the possibilities.

Some of the exercises in this lesson will serve as a review of material you covered earlier and some will add to your skills of procedures.

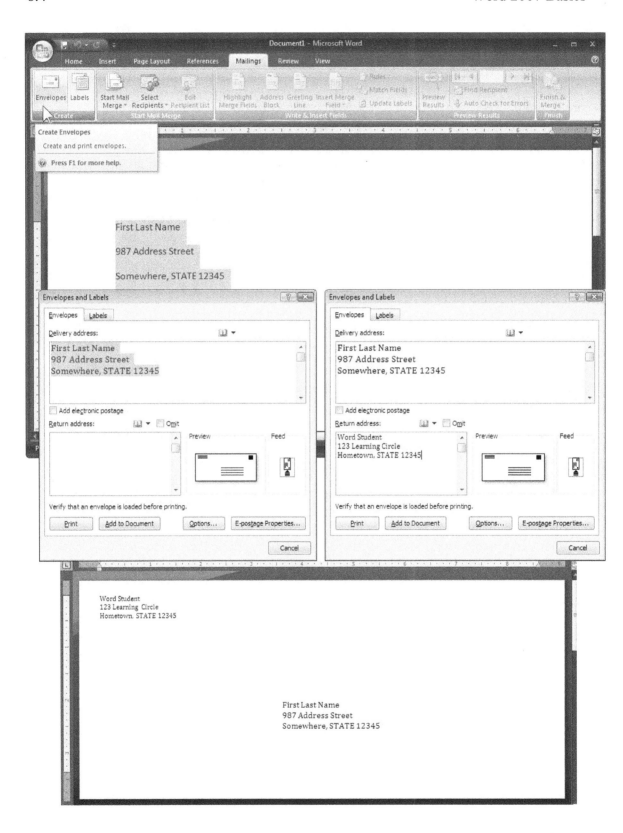

Printing Envelopes

You will often use Word to prepare letters. Word offers a quick way to also print envelopes. The exercise here shows you the approach. Printers vary a great deal. How you load an envelope into you own printer may be different from what is described here.

First prepare a letter. There is no need for the body of the letter since here you are only concerned with the address.

Exercise:

* Open Word.
* Type the address of the recipient of the letter. You can use the example shown on the left.
* Select all lines of the address – do not select any blank lines.
* Click the **Mailings** tab.
* In the **Create** group click **Envelopes**. See picture at left. The **Envelopes and Labels** dialog opens with the text you selected already in the **Delivery address:** box.
* Enter your return address in the **Return address:** box.

The **Options** command opens the **Envelope Options** dialog with two tabs to allow you to select the correct envelope size and the way the envelope needs to feed into your printer. The exercise here does not go into those options.

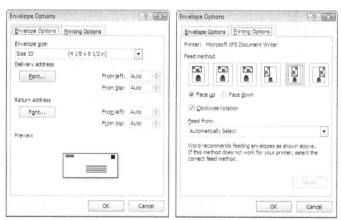

The next step normally is to click **Print**. Here, just to see what the envelope would look like, you will use another option.

* Click **Add to Document**. (Click **No** in the dialog that asks if you want to save the return address as the default).

The document is modified to include a view of the envelope. See the picture at left. Note that Word took care of the details to place the return address into the upper left area and to nicely place the recipient address properly on the envelope.

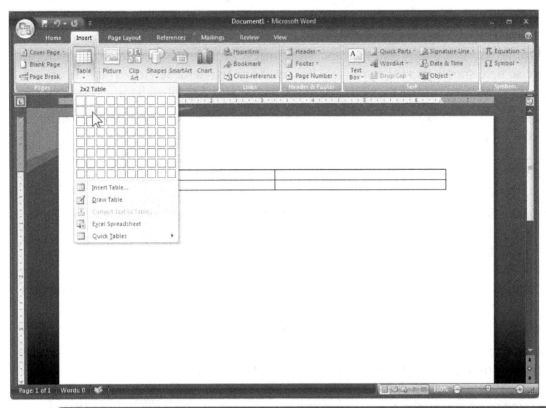

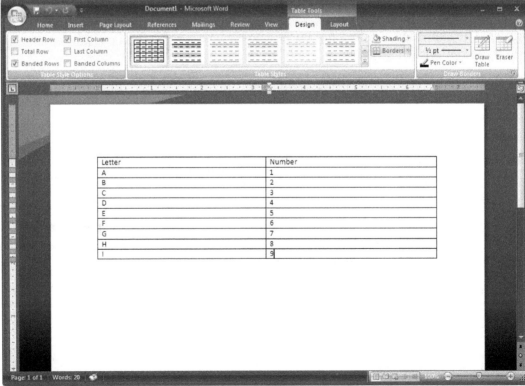

Creating a Data Set – Word Document

In order to merge data into a document you need some data. For mail merge to operate properly, the data must be in a well-structured form that Word can read and understand. Such data can be in the form of an Excel spreadsheet, an Access database file, in several other data formats or simply a Word document containing a table.

In this next exercise, you will set up a document as a source of data to be merged into another document. This will be a table with two columns containing just letters and numbers. The columns will be headed with "label" words that Word will later use as the field names.

Exercise:

* Start Word.
* Click the **Insert** tab.
* Click **Table**.
* In the gallery move the pointer from the top left corner over one box and down one box so that four boxes are highlighted. Notice how the table appears underneath in the document.
* Click. See the illustration at left for guidance. The 2x2 table will be created and the cursor will be in the first cell.
* Type the following word: `letter`.
* Press the **Tab** key. Note that the word is capitalized and the cursor moved to the second cell.
* Type: `number`.
* Press **Tab**. Again the word is capitalized and the cursor moved to the next cell, this time to the first cell in the second row.
* Type the letter **a**, press **Tab**, type **1**, press **Tab**.
* Note that the letter is capitalized and after the last Tab a new row of cells has been added.
* Continue entering letters and numbers until you have done "I 9".
* Click the **Office Button**.
* Click **Save As**. The **Save As** dialog opens.
* If you still have your **exercise documents** folder, double-click it. If you no longer have that folder, create it again. Need help? See page 3.7.
* In the **File Name:** box enter **data**.
* Click **Save**.
* Close Word.

You now have a Word document containing a data table. In this procedure you have also learned how the **Tab** key is used to add additional rows to a table.

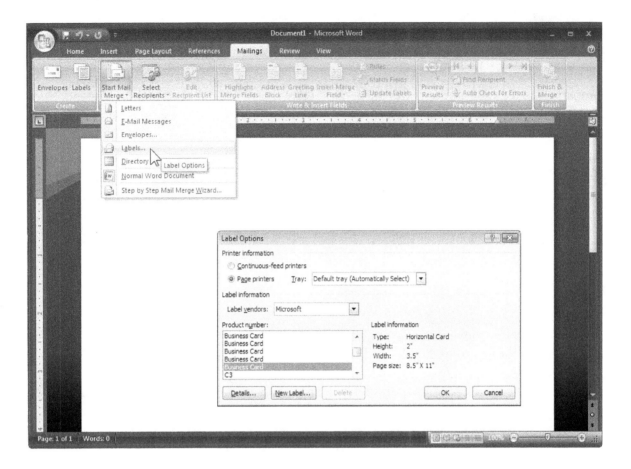

Setup Labels

Now an exercise to explore the feature of Word for preparing labels or business cards.

Word contains information for a large number of commercial label and card products. There is also generic data for some common and similar products.

The first step is to define the format of the stock that you will be printing on. Rather than using a commercial item, the exercise here uses generic Microsoft data.

Exercise:

* Start Word.
* Click the **Mailings** tab.
* In the **Start Mail Merge** group click **Start Mail Merge**.
* In the drop-down menu click **Labels...**
* In the **Label Options** dialog scroll down in the **Product Number:** box to the last **Business Card** entry. (This is for cards on 8.5x11 inch paper.)
* Click **OK**. Nothing much will seem to have happened.

You now have set up the formatting for business cards, each 2 inches high and 3.5 inches wide, 2 across, 5 down the page. The cursor is located in the first card space. Next add some fixed material.

Insert a Picture

It is normal to have some static or fixed information on the document that will then also use the variable data from an outside source. For fun and review this exercise adds a picture to each card.

Exercise:

* ✳ Click the **Insert** tab.
* ✳ Click **Picture**. The Insert Picture dialog opens.
* ✳ Browse to the pictures folder in **Documents - WB_Practice Files – File management**.
* ✳ Click on **Portrait of Lady G**.
* ✳ Click **Insert**.

This picure is placed into the card space. Iit is way too large, so some picture manipulation is in order. The picture is already selected and the **Picture Tools** tab has been added to the Ribbon and is active.

Exercise:

* ✳ In the **Arrange** group click **Text Wrapping**.
* ✳ Click on Square (see illustration at left).
* ✳ In the Size group click on the **Dialog Box Launcher**, .
* ✳ Change the value in the **Height:** box to **1**.
* ✳ Click **Close**. The picture changes to a smaller size.
* ✳ Click to the right of the top right corner of the picture to place the cursor.
* ✳ Type: **Participant**. Press **Enter** three times and type: **Save the Wildlife**.

You now have some fixed material on the card.

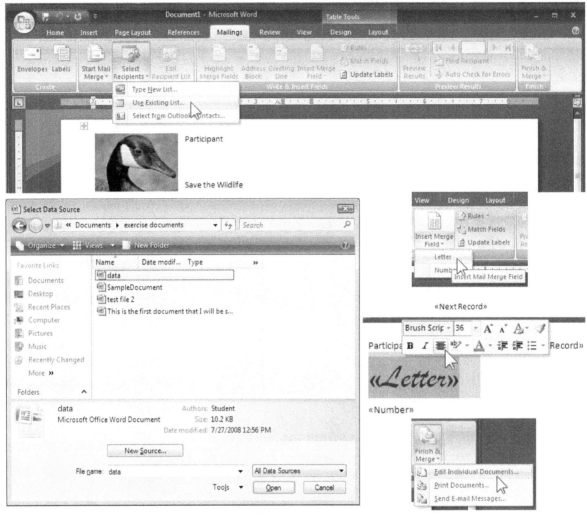

Merging Data

Now you are finally ready to merge some data into your card document. This exercise also sets formatting for the imported information.

Exercise:

* Click the **Mailings** tab.
* In the **Start Mail Merge** group click **Select Recipients**.
* Click **Use Existing List**. The Select Data Source dialog opens.
* Click **Documents** in the navigation pane.
* Double-click **exercise documents**.
* Click on **data**.
* Click Open. You will now see **<<Next record>>** in each of the other card locations.
* Click below " Participant"in the first (top left) card location.
* In the Write & Insert Fields group click on **Insert Merge Field ▼**. Click on the ▼.
* Two options are displayed: Letter and Number. These are the column headings from your data table!
* Click **Letter**. Note the addition of **<<Letter>>** in the document.
* Press **Enter**.
* Again click on **Insert Merge Field ▼**. Click on **Number** this time.
* Press **Enter**.
* Now select <<Letter>> - be carefull to select the << and >> as well.
* Use the Mini Toolbar to change the font to **Brush Script MT**, the size to **36**, and click on ☰ to center the text.
* Select <<Number>> - carefully again to get all of the symbols – and change the size to **20**, and center the text.
* In the **Write & Insert Fields** group click **Update Labels**. The fixed data, the fields and their formatting are all copied to the other card positions.
* In the **Finish** group click **Finish & Merge ▼**. Click on the ▼.
* Click **Edit Individual Document...**
* In the **Merge to New Document** dialog **All** is already selected, click **OK**.

A new document, Labels1, opens showing the cards and the merged data. You are now ready to print this. Scroll down to the bottom of the new document. Note that the last, tenth, card has no merged data. The data in the table has just nine sets, so the last card only shows the fixed material.

For real cards you would now be ready to print them. Here just enjoy your feat.

Lesson Eight Review Questions

A. How do you print an address on an envelope?

1. You make a new document and set the margins to four inches from the left and two inches from the top, type the address and print it.
2. You select the text of the address and click Envelopes in the Create group on the Mailings tab.
3. You use cut and paste – just like in Kindergarten.

{For answer, see page 8.5]

B. How do you insert the recipient's name in your party announcement?

1. No big deal, you just type in the first name, print it, replace the name with the next recipient, print it and so on.
2. You type the names on separate lines and use Show/Hide to only show one name at a time.
3. You make a table with the names in a separate document and use Mail Merge on the Mailings tab.

[For answer, see page 8.13]

C. How do you insert a picture in your party announcement?

1. You order enough copies and paste them in – just like in Kindergarten.
2. You select WordArt on the Insert tab.
3. You place the cursor where you want the picture and click Picture in the Illustrations group on the Insert tab.

[For answer, see page 6.5 or 8.11]

Answers: A – 2, B – 3, C – 3.

9. Finish

This last chapter is not another lesson, just a wind-up with some cleaning chores and some useful information.

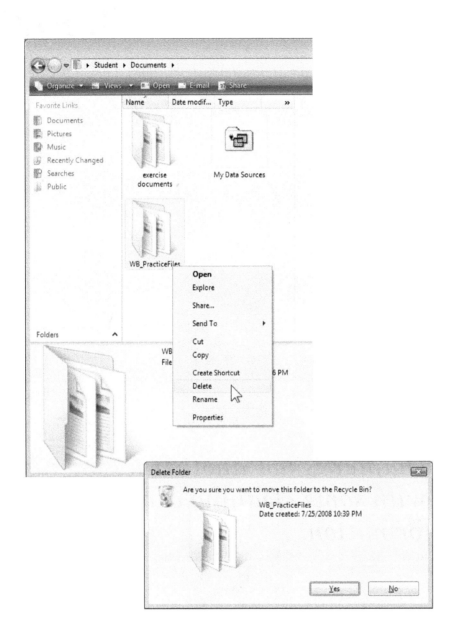

Cleanup

Now that you have completed this book, and surely repeated many of the exercises, there is just a small chore left to do. Once you are comfortable using Word and don't feel the need to practice using the files you created and downloaded, you can clean up your computer to delete this material and make room for your own, more important files.

So here is one last exercise to do just that.

Exercise:

* ✱ Click **Start**.
* ✱ Click **Documents**. [Windows XP user: click **My Documents**.]
* ✱ Find the **WB_PracticeFiles** folder.
* ✱ Right-click it and click **Delete**
* ✱ Answer **Yes** in the **Delete Folder** dialog.
* ✱ Find the **exercise documents** folder.
* ✱ Right-click it and click **Delete**
* ✱ Answer **Yes** in the **Delete Folder** dialog.

You may find a folder named **My Data Sources**. Word may have created that in the label making exercise. Leave this folder on your system for future use.

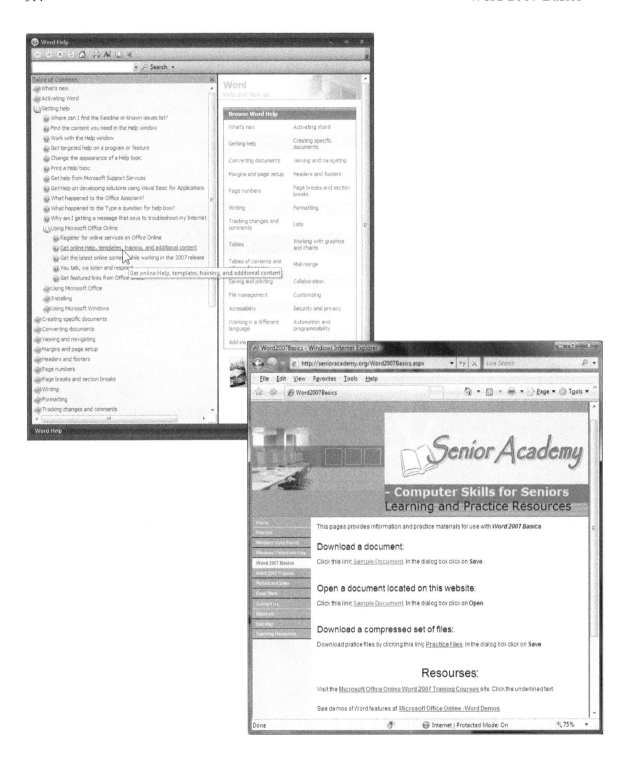

Additional Learning Resources

You have now completed this manual. Surely, you will have some questions, and hopefully you are eager to learn even more skills for the use of this very powerful program, Word.

Microsoft provides powerful help within the program and even more online on the Internet.

Exercise:

* Start Word.
* Click the **Help** command, .
* If the table of contents is not open, click the **Show Table of Contents** command.
* Click **Getting help** to expand.
* Scroll down to **Using Microsoft Word Online** and click to expand.
* Click Get online help…
* Scroll down the right pane to the bottom and click **Office Online**. Your browser opens and takes you to the frequently updated Microsoft Office Online home page.
* Click the **Help and How-to** tab.
* On the left, the navigation pane note the offerings of training courses, demos, and other help.
* Explore the training course catalog and the demos.

There is a great deal of help available on this site. You can spend many hours exploring, seeing demos, and taking training courses.

You might find getting to some of these sites a bit faster by visiting **senioracademy.org** and clicking on the **Word 2007 Basics** link in the navigation pane.

A. Glossary of Terms

A

Align – to set text in a specified manner – flush with the left or right margin, centered, or justified – flush with both margins.

AutoCorrect – a Word feature for correcting mistyped words as they are typed.

AutoFormat – a Word feature to produce, for example, bulleted or numbered lists.

B

Break – a space between lines, paragraphs or pages.

Bullet – a mark in front of text lines in a list.

C

Caps lock – A key on the keyboard, above the left Shift key, that toggles CAPITAL text on and off.

Center – to set text so it is evenly spaced between the margins.

Clipboard – A hidden memory location for storing copied and cut items. Can be made visible in Word.

Column – text column – text set in separate groups of lines that read from top to bottom.

Copy – to make a copy of selected text or another item. The copy command stores the copied item on the clipboard.

Cursor – The icon showing the "text insertion point". Normally a flashing, vertical line.

Cut – to remove a selected item. The item is stored on the clipboard for later use.

D

Dash – a line-shaped character, hyphen, em dash, en dash.

Default – the setting or option used by the program when no other setting has been specified by the user.

Dialog box – a special window to select specific options or receive specific information.

Drop cap – a letter or word set in a larger size at the beginning of a paragraph.

F

Flash drive – a storage device for information that retains the data even when no power is applied.

Font – set of shapes for characters.

G

Gallery – a pictorial collection of available commands or options.

Gridline – a faint set of lines (non-printing) to assist in placing items.

Group – a set of related commands on the Ribbon.

I

Insert – to place an item into a document such as a picture.

J

Justify – to set text so both the left and right edges are flush with the margins.

L

Landscape – page orientation with the long side horizontal.

Left align – To set text so it is flush with the left margin.

List – A collection of text items arranged in a list.

M

Margin – the white space at the edges, top and bottom of the page.

Mini Toolbar – a small dialog with formatting options, pops up when text is selected.

Mouse – a peripheral device for entering location and action information into the computer.

N

Navigation key – a keyboard key for navigating within a document. These include the arrow keys, Home, End, Page Up, Page Down and others.

O

Office button – the button to open a menu of common commands.

Open – to load a document into Word or another application. To launch an application.

P

Page layout – the placement of the text on a page.

Paste – to place a copy of an item stored on the clipboard at a specified location.

Persistent memory – a storage device that retains information even when powered off. Such devices include hard drives which retain information magnetically, CD and DVD discs which store information optically or mechanically, flash drives which store information with electric charges.

Pointer – the movable icon directed by the mouse.

Portrait – page orientation with the long side vertical.

R

Ribbon – the prominent location of commands at the top of the Word window.

Right align – to set text so it is flush with the right margin.

Ruler – a marked scale at the top and/or left side to permit judging the position or extent of text.

S

Save – the process of copying information from the (volatile) computer memory to a medium that retains the information. Such media include hard drives, CD and DVD discs, flash drives.

Shape – a graphical design element. Word provides a large number of predefined shapes.

Size – height of text characters. Normally expressed in points – 72 points = 1 inch.

Style – a set of properties for paragraphs.

T

Tab – a division of the Ribbon.

Table – information displayed in a two-dimensional array, usually separated by lines.

Text Insertion Point – the location in a window where characters typed on the keyboard appear. Usually marked with a "cursor", a flashing, vertical line, or highlighted text which will be replaced by the next character entered on the keyboard.

Thumbnail – a small picture of an item.

U

USB port – an input/output port used extensively on computers, peripheral equipment, cameras, and other electronic devices.

V

Volatile memory – the high-speed computer memory that is sustained only while power is applied. When power is turned off the contents of this memory is lost.

W

WordArt – a set of commands in Word to manipulate the shape and color of text.

Z

Zoom – to control the magnification of the text on the monitor.

B. File Management Exercises

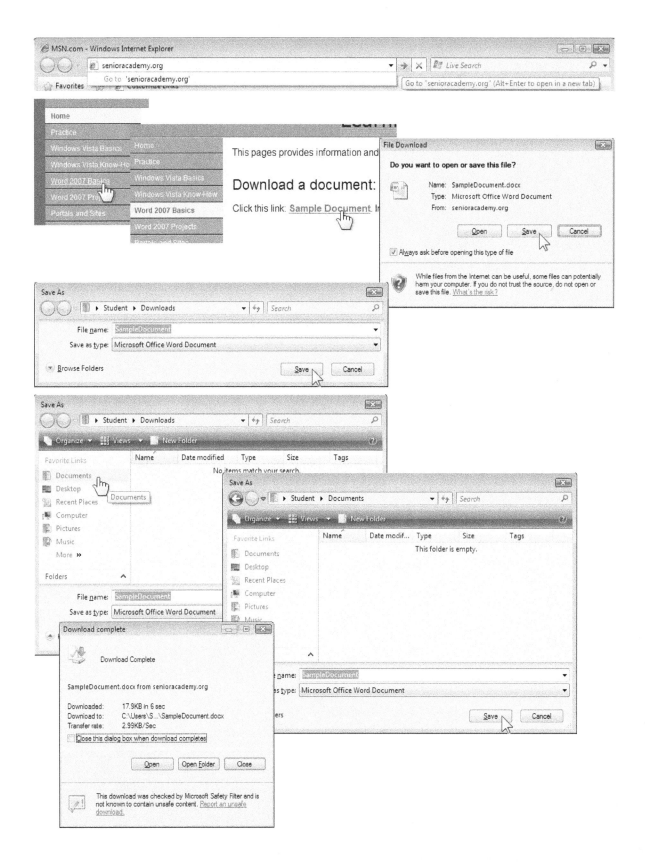

Download a Sample File from a Website

Websites often provide files which you may download to your computer. The website "SeniorAcademy.org" provides material for use with this course. For the first lesson exercises, download a single file.

Proceed as follows:

[Note to users of Word 2007 on XP: Turn to page C-3]

Exercise:

* Click **Start**.
* Click on **Internet** – usually very near the top of the Start menu.
* Click in the address bar.
* Type the website address: `senioracademy.org`.
* Press **Enter** or click the "go to" button, [→], to the right of the address bar.
* On the Senior Academy website, find the [Word 2007 Basics] listing in the navigation bar at the left and click it.
* In the **Download a Document** section click the **Sample Document** link.
* In the **File Download** dialog click **Save**.
* The Save As dialog opens and presents a location, most likely **Downloads**. Expand the dialog by clicking **Browse Folders** if needed.
* Click **Documents** in the navigation pane.
* Accept the file name ("SampleDocument") by clicking **Save**.
* You may see a **Download complete** dialog. Close the dialog by clicking **Close**.

You have now downloaded a file from the Internet website and saved it in your Documents folder.

Click this link: Sample Document. In the dialog box click on **Save**.

Open a document located on this website:

Click this link: Sample Document. In the dialog box click on **Open**.

Download a compressed set of files:

Download pratice files by clicking this link: **Practice Files**. In the dialog box click on **Save**.

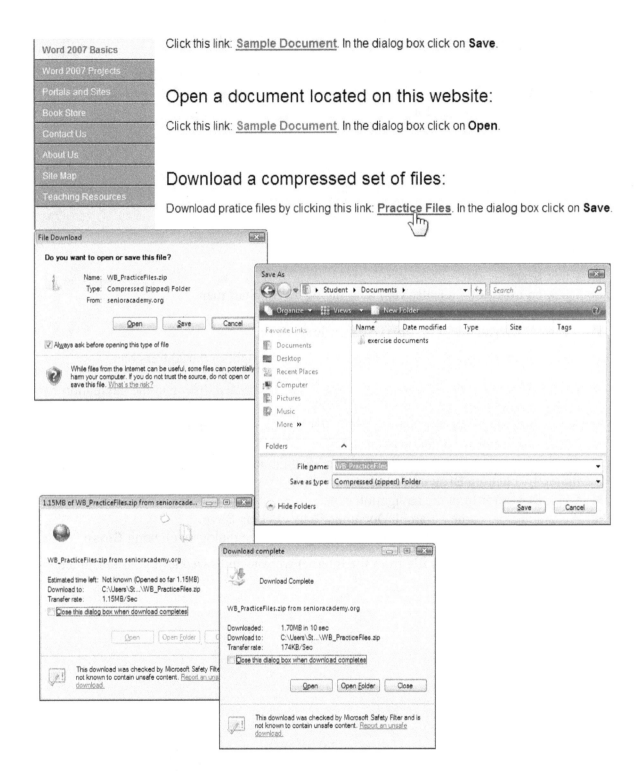

Download a Compressed File from a Website

To install more practice files on your computer, download a set in the form of a compressed file. Compressing, or "zipping," allows a group of files and folder to be combined into one file. The compressed file is much smaller than the sum of the file sizes. This takes less space, and much more importantly, will allow the material to be downloaded much faster than would be the case with individual files.

The "zip" file that you will be downloading is much larger that the single file you downloaded before, so it will take a bit longer. On most high speed Internet connections it will take a couple of seconds or so.

You may refer to the previous pages for some of the illustrations.

Proceed as follows;

Exercise:

* ✱ Click **Start**.
* ✱ Click on **Internet** – usually very near the top of the Start menu.
* ✱ Click in the address bar.
* ✱ Type the website address: **senioracademy.org**.
* ✱ Press **Enter** or click the "go to" button, ➡, to the right of the address bar.
* ✱ Note: Since you visited this site before, your browser will show the address as soon as you type the first few letters. Click on the address in the drop-down menu so you will not need to retype the whole address.
* ✱ On the Senior Academy website, find the [Word 2007 Basics] listing in the navigation bar at the left and click it.
* ✱ In the **Download compressed set of files** section click the **Practice Files** link.
* ✱ In the **File Download** dialog click **Save**.
* ✱ The Save As dialog opens and presents a location, most likely **Downloads**. Expand the dialog by clicking **Browse Folders** if needed.
* ✱ Click **Documents** in the navigation pane.
* ✱ Accept the file name ("WB_PracticeFiles.zip") by clicking **Save**.
* ✱ You will see a File Download dialog. It will show **Download Complete** in a few seconds. Close the dialog by clicking **Close**.

You have now downloaded a compressed file from the Internet website and saved it in your Documents folder.

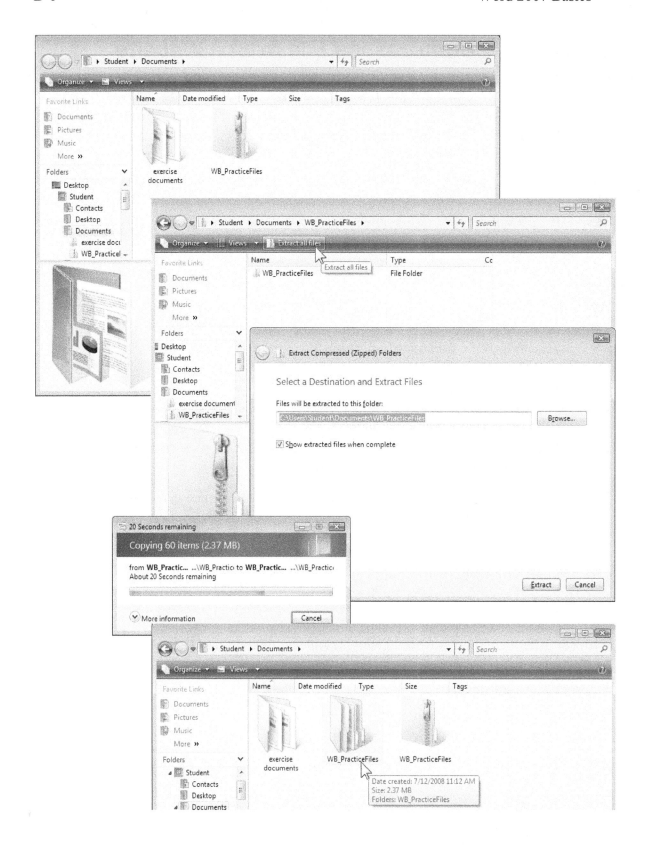

Expand a Compressed File

You can tell a compressed file by the icon with a zipper on a folder – normally these files have a ".zip" name extension. To restore the files so you can use them normally, proceed as follows:

Exercise:

* Locate the file **WB_PracticeFiles.zip** in your **Documents** folder. Double-click it.
* Notice on the tool bar there is an Extract option, . Click it.
* You get a chance to assign a name to the new folder. Accept the default name which is the same as the name of the zip file.
* After a short operation, you will have a new folder with the expanded contents of the zip file.

You will have a new folder in **Documents** with the name **WB_PracticeFiles**. Inside that folder there will be another folder by the same name. Inside that folder you will find a folder named **File Management** and eleven document files. You are now ready for more exercises.

Still in **Documents** is the zip file that you downloaded. You will not need this file and may delete it.

You will be using some of these files in several lessons. Just for fun, and as review practice of skills you already know, go on to the next pages for some file management exercises.

C. Notes for Users with Windows XP

Word 2007 looks and operates pretty much the same on Windows XP as it does on Windows Vista. The most noticeable differences appear when file services are invoked such as open, save, insert. These differences are illustrated in this section.

In Windows XP the folder for your files is called "My Documents." This folder also contains the folder for your pictures, "My Pictures," and the folder for your music files, "My Music."

In the following pages portions of the material from the lesson chapters are repeated with the wording appropriate for Windows XP and with illustrations showing the windows as they appear on a Windows XP computer.

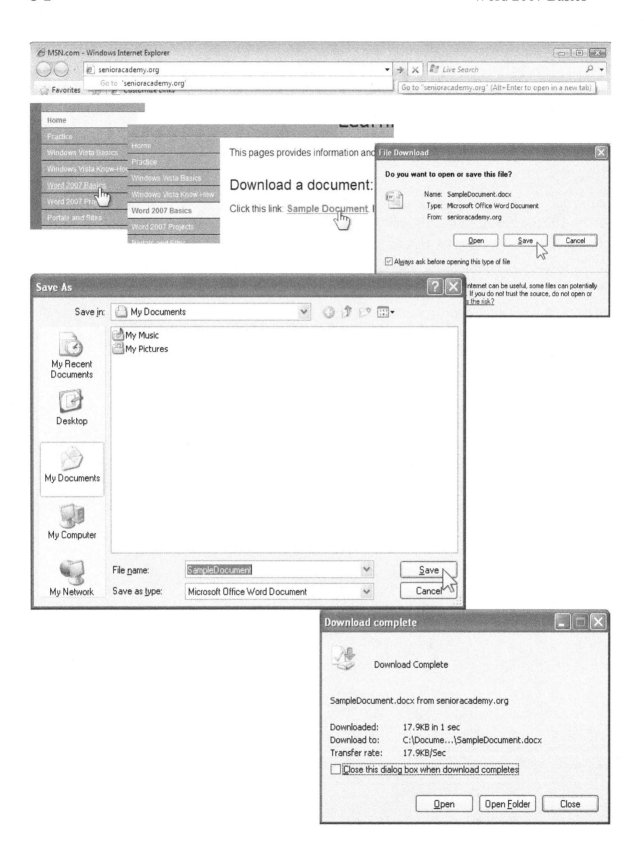

Download a Sample File from a Website

Proceed as follows:

Exercise:

* ❋ Click **Start**.
* ❋ Click on **Internet** – usually very near the top of the Start menu.
* ❋ After the browser has opened, click in the address bar.
* ❋ Type the website address: **senioracademy.org**.
* ❋ Press **Enter** or click the "go to" button, →, to the right of the address bar.
* ❋ On the Senior Academy website, find the Word 2007 Basics listing in the navigation bar at the left and click it.
* ❋ In the Download a Document section click the **Sample Document** link.
* ❋ In the **File Download** dialog click **Save**.
* ❋ The Save As dialog opens and presents a "Save in" location, most likely **My Documents**. If the location is not My Documents, click on **My Documents** in the navigation pane at the left.
* ❋ Accept the file name ("SampleDocument") by clicking **Save**.
* ❋ You may see a **Download complete** dialog. Close the dialog by clicking **Close**.

You have now downloaded a file from the Internet website and saved it in your My Documents folder.

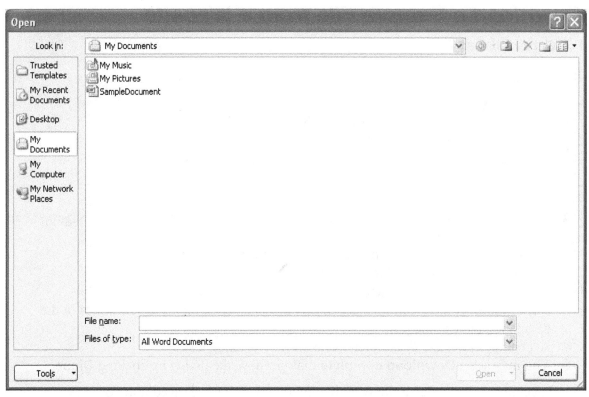

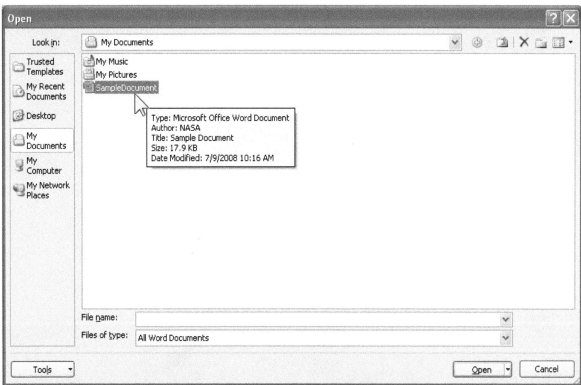

Opening a Document

 To open, or load, a document, you use the **Open** command located in the Office menu. You reach the Office menu by clicking the Office button in the upper left corner. When you click the **Open** command button the Open dialog is displayed. This is like a "service" of Windows Explorer. You can use all the normal methods for maneuvering, "browsing," in the Open dialog to find the source document.

In the left pane of the Open dialog you select an item, disk or folder, by a single click. The contents of that item is then displayed in the contents pane on the right. To open a folder in the right pane, double-click it.

To open a document when it is displayed in the right, contents, pane, you may double-click it or just click it and then click the **Open** button at the lower right of the Open dialog window.

Exercise:

* Click the **Office** button.
* Click the **Open** button.
* The Open dialog likely shows the contents of your My Documents folder. If it does not click **My Documents** in the navigation pane on the left.
* You will see your documents in the contents pane. In the illustration at the left there are two folders, My Music and My Pictures, and just one document in the folder. Double-click **SampleDocument** – or click it (to select it) and click **Open**.

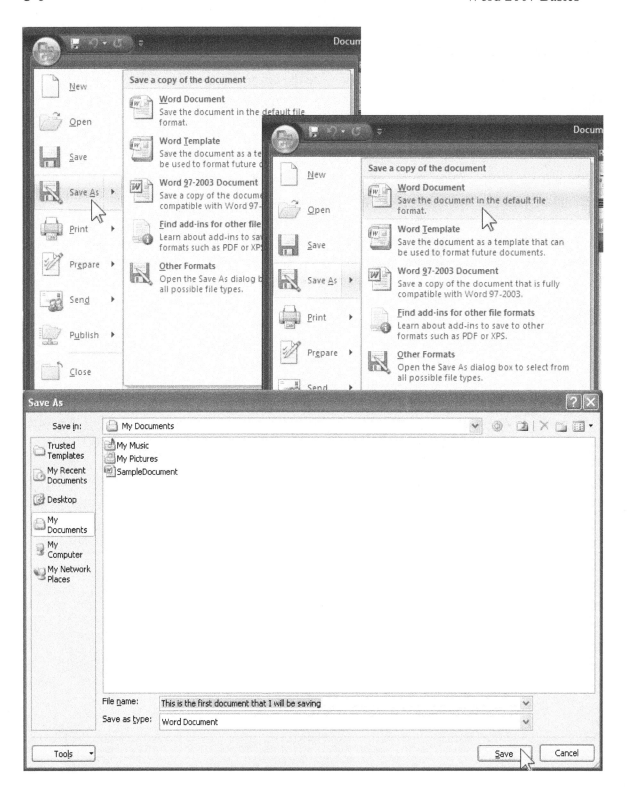

Creating a Document

Exercise:

* ✱ Start Word.
* ✱ Enter some text. If you don't know what to type, here is a suggestion: **This is the first document that I will be saving**.
* ✱ Click the **Office** button,
* ✱ Move the pointer down to the **Save As** command. It will change color and a menu will appear in the right pane.
* ✱ Click **Word Document** in the right pane.

This will bring up the Save As dialog. It will look similar to the picture on the left.

At the top is the "Save in" box. This is where you specify the storage location for the document. By default it will show My Documents. This is where you will store most of your documents. When you have many documents, you will want to store them in a folder, or a sub-folder, within the My Document folder. You will learn more about that shortly. For now, the My Documents folder is the right place. Near the bottom is the **File name:** box. This is a text entry box where you specify the name for the document. Word uses part of the first line of the document as the default name. You can overtype it. Here just accept the default name.

There is a Save as type: control. Accept the default Word Document setting.

Exercise:

* ✱ Click the **Save** command in the **Save As** dialog window.
* ✱ Close Word. It will close without asking to confirm saving because you just did.

You have created a document. It is stored in the My Documents folder. Its name is **This is the first document that I will be saving**. Yes, all of that is the document's name.

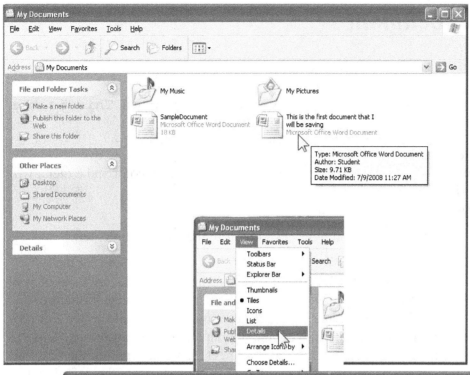

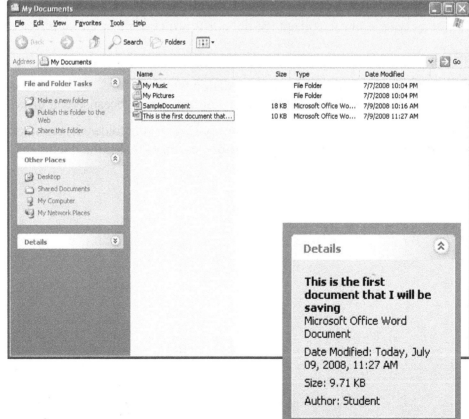

Finding a Saved Document

Did you really just save a document? Open it back up as described in the following exercise.

Exercise:

* Click **Start**.
* Click **My Documents**.

Windows Explorer opens showing the contents of the My Documents folder. On your computer at home there may be many other items in this folder. Here there is just the file you downloaded from the Internet earlier and the newly created file in addition to the two folders, My Music and My Pictures.

Exercise:

* Click **View** in the Menu bar.
* Click **Details**.

Notice that most likely not all of the name will show. This is one of the reasons why it is good to give documents short names.

Exercise:

* Click on the name of the document you created.

* In the navigation pane click | Details ⏬ |
* You may need to scroll down in the navigation pane to see all of the information.

Notice that all sorts of details are listed in the details section of the navigation pane.

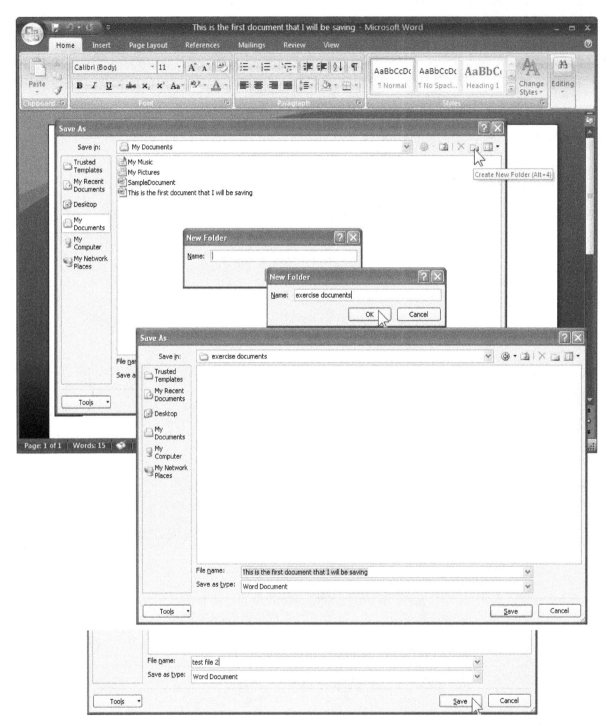

Saving a Document

Exercise:

* Start the save process as before: Click the **Office** button, click **Save As** (You don't really have to click on Word Document, this is the default.)

The Save As dialog looks similar to Windows Explorer because it is Windows Explorer, just with a different "hat" on.

Create a New Folder

In the Save As dialog there is a command icon to create a new folder, . This works exactly the same way that it works in the normal Windows Explorer window.

Exercise:

* Click the **Create New Folder** icon on the tool bar in the Save As dialog window.
* A New Folder dialog opens. Enter the name of the new folder in the **Name:** box. Use: **exercise documents**.
* Click **OK**.
* The contents of the new folder will be shown. It is empty, of course.
* The current name of the document is shown in the File name: box. The name will be selected so you can just type in the new name. Use: **test file 2**.
* Click **Save**.

The file is saved. Notice that the Word window title bar now shows the new name.

Exercise:

* Close Word.

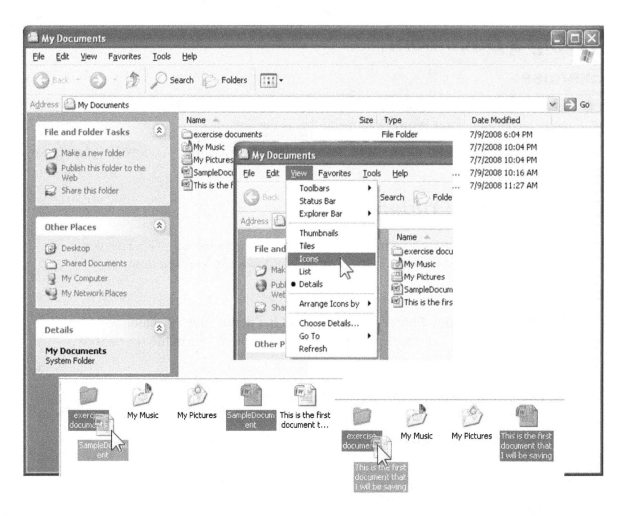

Review – Moving Files

In the following exercise you will move files by dragging them to the destination folder. When dragging files within a drive (such as the C: drive), that is, from one location on the drive, to another location on the same drive, files are moved. Moving a file means that it is removed from the source location and placed into the destination location.

You will now move the file you downloaded from the Internet and the first file that you created from the Documents folder to the exercise documents folder that you made within the Documents folder.

Exercise:

* Click **Start**.
* Click **My Documents**.
* Change the view of the contents pane to large icons. Click the ▼ next to **View**, then click **Large Icons**.
* Find the file **SampleDocument** and drag it to the **exercise documents** folder.
* Find the file **This is the first ...** and drag it to the **exercise documents** folder.
* Drag it to the **exercise documents** folder.

Why did you change the view to large icons? Because large items are easier to drag and the large folder icon presents a larger "target"!

Click this link: <u>Sample Document</u>. In the dialog box click on **Save**.

Open a document located on this website:

Click this link: <u>Sample Document</u>. In the dialog box click on **Open**.

Download a compressed set of files:

Download pratice files by clicking this link: **<u>Practice Files</u>**. In the dialog box click on **Save**.

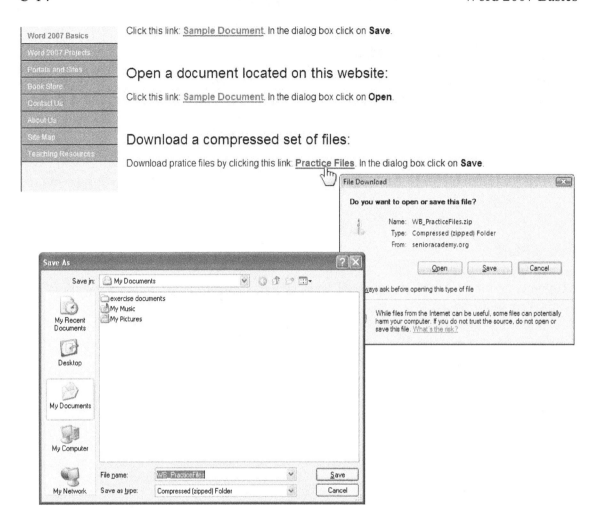

Download a Compressed File from a Website

To get more practice files to your computer, download a set in the form of a compressed file. Compressing, or "zipping," allows a group of files and folders to be combined into one file. The compressed file is much smaller than the sum of the file sizes. This takes less space, and much more importantly, will allow the material to be downloaded much faster than would be the case with individual files.

The "zip" file that you will be downloading is much larger that the single file you downloaded before, so it will take a bit longer. On most high speed Internet connections it will take a couple of seconds or so.

You may refer to the previous pages for some of the illustrations.

Proceed as follows;

Exercise:

* Click **Start**.
* Click on **Internet** – usually very near the top of the Start menu.
* Click in the address bar.
* Type the website address: **senioracademy.org**.
* Press **Enter** or click the "go to" button, , to the right of the address bar.
* Note: Since you visited this site before, your browser will show the address as soon as you type the first few letters. Click on the address in the drop-down menu so you will not need to retype the whole address.
* On the Senior Academy website, find the listing in the navigation bar at the left and click it.
* In the **Download compressed set of files** section click the **Practice Files** link.
* In the **File Download** dialog click **Save**.
* The Save As dialog opens and presents a location, most likely **My Documents**. If it is other than My Documents Click **My Documents** in the navigation pane.
* Accept the file name ("WB_PracticeFiles.zip") by clicking **Save**.
* You will see a File Download dialog. It will show **Download Complete** in a few seconds. Close the dialog by clicking **Close**.

You have now downloaded a compressed file from the Internet website and saved it in your Documents folder.

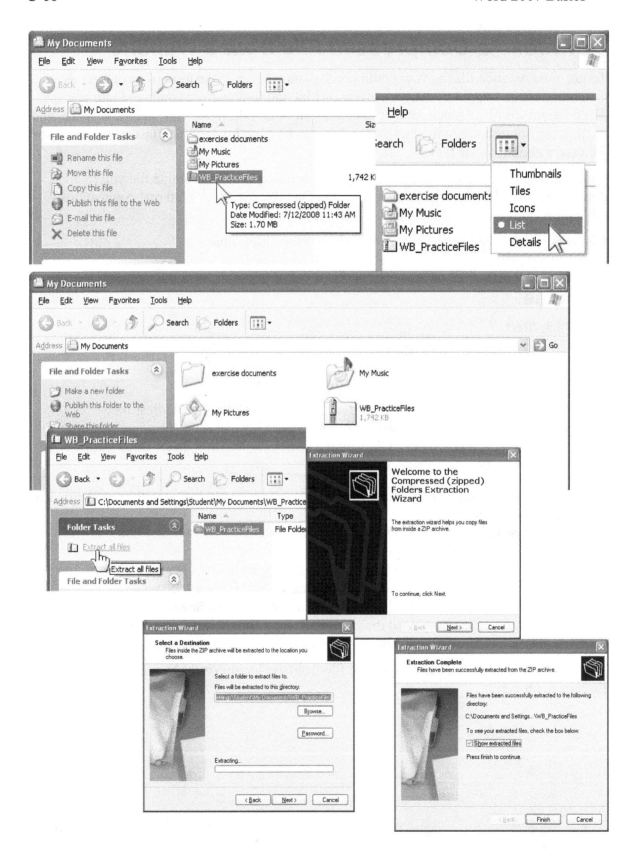

Expand a Compressed File

You can tell a compressed file by the icon with a zipper on a folder – normally these files have a ".zip" name extension. To restore the files so you can use them normally, proceed as follows:

Exercise:

* Open the My Documents folder (Click **Start**, then **My Documents**).
* Change the view to Tiles so you can more easily identity the zip file.
* Locate the file **WB_PracticeFiles.zip** in your Documents folder. Double-click it.
* Click on **WB_PracticeFiles** in the new contents pane.
* Notice **Folder Tasks** on the left. Click on **Extract all files**.
* In the Extraction Wizard dialog click **Next**.
* You get a chance to assign a name to the new folder. Accept the default name which is the same as the name of the zip file. Click **Next**.
* On the last dialog click **Finish**.
* After a short operation, you will have a new folder with the expanded contents of the zip file.

You will have a new folder in **My Documents** with the name **WB_PracticeFiles**. Inside that folder there will be another folder by the same name. Inside that folder you will find a folder named **File Management** and eleven document files. You are now ready for more exercises.

Still in **My Documents** is the zip file that you downloaded. You will not need this file and may delete it.

Just for fun, and as review practice of skills you already know, go on to the next pages for some file management exercises.

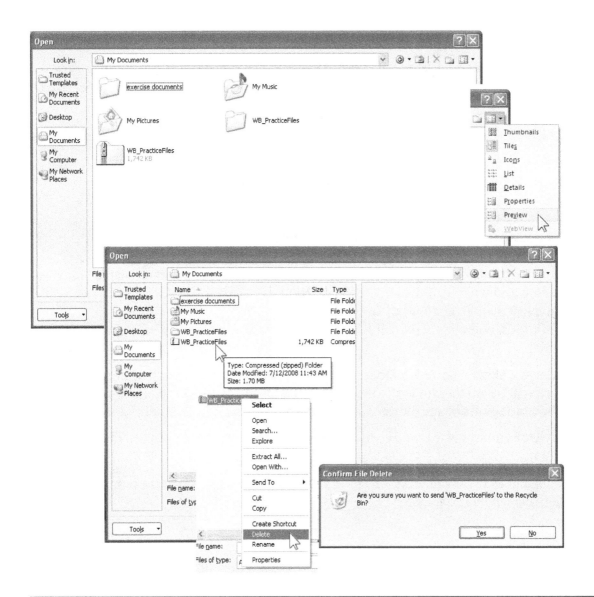

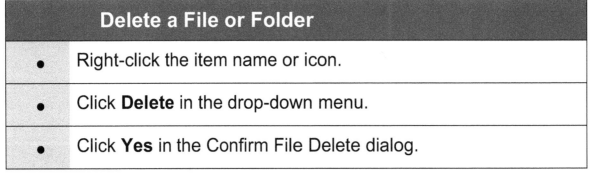

	Delete a File or Folder
•	Right-click the item name or icon.
•	Click **Delete** in the drop-down menu.
•	Click **Yes** in the Confirm File Delete dialog.

Organizing Files and Folders

The Open dialog should resemble the top illustration at the left. On your own computer you will also see your other files. Here we are concerned only with the ones shown in the illustration.

Exercise:

* ✳ Open Word. You may do so by clicking the Word shortcut on the Desktop.
* ✳ Click the **Office Button**.
* ✳ Click **Open**.
* ✳ Click the **Views** icon on the right side of the Open dialog window.
* ✳ Click **Preview** in the menu. This opens the Preview pane on the right side.

Deleting a File or Folder

You no longer need the file you downloaded from the Senior Academy website since you have extracted its contents. This file is called WB_PracticeFiles.zip, the extension may not be shown, but you can recognize it by the zipper.

Exercise:

* ✳ Hover the pointer on the **WB_PracticeFiles** icon with the zipper. Note that it is described as a "Compressed (zipped) Folder".
* ✳ Right-click on the icon or name.
* ✳ In the drop-down menu click **Delete**.
* ✳ In the **Confirm File Delete** dialog click **Yes** to move the file to the Recycle Bin.

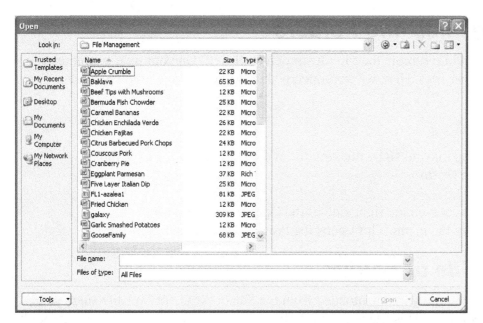

Create a New Folder

•	Browse to the folder where you want to create a new one.
•	Click the **Create New Folder** command.
•	Type the name of the new folder (into the text entry box).
•	Press **Enter** or click **OK**.

Creating a New Folder

Still using the Open dialog to practice file management, you will now move around in the practice files folder and create a couple of new folders. The folder File Management contains 47 items; some are pictures and some are recipes. These files clearly are not well organized. For the next exercises, you will create two new folders and move the files into the appropriate new folder.

Exercise:

- Double-click the **WB_PacticeFiles** icon or name. The contents of the folder is now displayed in the contents pane.
- Double-click the **File Management** folder to display the contents of that folder.
- Click the **Create New Folder** icon (right end of tool bar). A New Folder dialog opens with a text box for the name of the folder.
- Type: **`recipes`** as the name of the new folder.
- Press **Enter** or click **OK**. The new folder is created and opened.
- Click the **Up One Level** icon to return to the File management folder.
- Click the **Create New Folder** icon to create another folder.
- Type: **`pictures`** as the name of this new folder.
- Press **Enter** or click **OK**. The new folder is created and opened.
- Click the **Up One Level** icon to return to the File management folder.

You now have two new folders to allow you to re-organize the files in this folder.

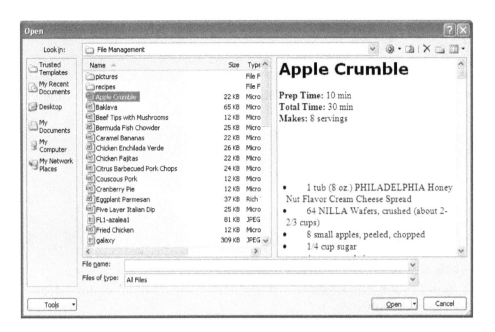

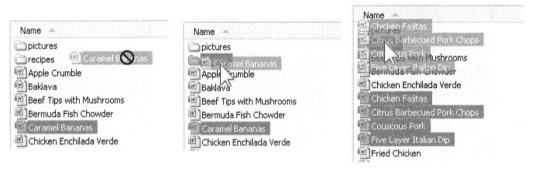

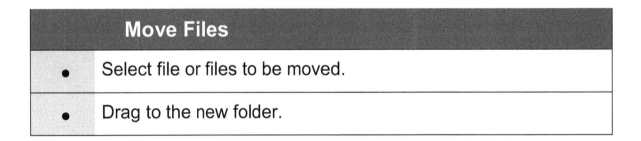

Move Files	
•	Select file or files to be moved.
•	Drag to the new folder.

Moving Files

To organize the files in the Files Management folder, move each file into the "recipe" folder if it is a recipe, into the "pictures" folder if it is a picture. For this exercise, use the Preview pane to identify the type of file you are dealing with.

NOTE: For this exercise you should have already done the following (in previous exercises): Start Word – launch the Open dialog – browse to the File Management folder (in WB_PracticeFiles) changed to Preview view and set the File of Type: to All Files.

Exercise:

* ✳ Click on a file. Note that the Preview pane shows the contents of the file.
* ✳ Drag the file to the appropriate folder. Note that until the pointer is over the folder icon
  or name there will be a "unavailable" icon, ⊘ superposed on the file name you are dragging. When the pointer is over the folder the normal pointer appears. This helps you to make sure that you are directing the file to the folder. It is up to you to make sure you get the correct folder. When you are on the correct folder, release the mouse button. The file will be moved.
* ✳ Repeat this several times more, dragging recipe files to the recipe folder and picture files to the picture folder.
* ✳ Identify several recipe files. Select these files by holding down the **Ctrl** key and click the files.
* ✳ Now place the pointer on any of the selected files and drag them (press the left mouse button) to the recipe folder.
* ✳ Continue until all files have been moved.

When you are finished check your work. You should have 10 pictures in the pictures folder. The other 37 files are recipe documents and should now be in the recipe folder.

NOTE: The method illustrated here is not as flexible as working in Windows Explorer. It does provide the advantage of being able to preview the files.

D. Index

align text..................................... 4.19
AutoCorrect.......................... 2.11, 2.13
AutoFormat 2.15
bold 2.7
box text..................................... 6.11
bullet list................................... 2.15
bullets 5.5
business cards............................ 8.9
center text.................................. 4.19
Close 1.7
columns 7.3
copy................................ 4.9, 4.13, 4.15
correcting error........................... 6.13
correcting text 2.9
create 3.3
create data set............................ 8.7
create folder 3.7
cursor................................... 4.2, 4.3
cut................................. 4.9, 4.13, 4.15
dash 6.18
date insert 6.3
Dialog Box Launcher 1.5
document create 3.3
drop cap..................................... 6.3
envelope 8.5
error correction........................... 6.13
find 5.11
find a document........................... 3.5
folder create 3.7
font 2.5
formatting marks.......................... 4.11
galleries 1.5
grammar check............................ 6.15
gridline 7.7
Home tab 1.5, 2.3

icon... 1.3
insert... 6.3
insert picture...................... 6.5, 8.11
insert shape................................ 6.7
italic.. 2.7
justify text.................................. 4.19
Key Tips..................................... 6.19
Label Option 8.9
labels 8.9
landscape................................... 7.5
layout... 7.3
left align 4.19
list.. 5.5
list sorting.................................. 5.5
Mail Merge.................................. 8.13
Mailings 8.3
margins....................................... 7.3
Mini Toolbar 4.7
move file 3.11
move text.................................... 4.17
navigation keys 1.13
New 1.7
numbered list...................... 2.15, 5.5
Office button 1.3, 1.7
Open 1.7, 1.9
open a document 3.5
open document 5.3
orientation 7.5
page layout 7.3
paragraph mark 4.11
paste 4.9, 4.13, 4.15
picture insert............................... 6.5, 8.11
Picture Tools 8.11
pointer 4.2, 4.3
portrait....................................... 7.5

print 7.5
Print 1.7
print envelope 8.5
Quick Access Toolbar 1.3
Quick launch 1.3
recent item 5.3
replace 5.13
Ribbon 1.3, 1.5
right align 4.19
right-click 4.9
ruler 7.7
save 3.3, 3.7
Save 1.7, 3.9
Save As 1.7, 3.9
select 4.5
shape insert 6.7
shortcut 1.3
shortcut keys 6.19
show/hide 4.11

size 2.5
sorting 5.5
spell check 6.15
styles 5.9
symbol insert 6.3
table 6.11, 8.7
table of contents 7.11
text align 4.19
text box 6.11
text color 4.7
text drag 4.17
text move 4.17
text select 4.5
thumbnail 7.7
underline 2.7
wavy underline 6.13
WordArt 6.9
zoom 7.7
Zoom 1.11

www.ingramcontent.com/pod-product-compliance
Lightning Source LLC
Chambersburg PA
CBHW080411060326
40689CB00019B/4203